THE

Quill

AND THE

Crow

VOLUME I

LILITH SAINTCROW

Dedication

For all new writers.
Never, ever doubt that you have a story to tell.

Table of Contents

Introduction

I have long made no secret of considering most books on writing useless. (The exceptions, of course, are Strunk & White's *Elements of Style* and Stephen King's *On Writing*, both of which are very low on bullshit.) Since I am about to inflict a collection of essays about that very subject on the world at large, I might as well explain my decision.

I dislike books on writing for the same reason I dislike self-help books: because people mistake the work of reading them for the actual work one must do to get better at writing, or better at dealing with yourself and your foibles. The ersatz jolt of advice wears off after a while, leaving the reader in exactly the same place, and they go searching for another high. Like the diet industry, if there was ever a "magic" formula, the entire edifice would tank overnight and several people would be out of jobs.

Why am I doing this? Simple. I've been asked by Readers and fellow writers to collect these essays for their reference. If it reaches beyond that small audience, please be warned: there are no goddamn shortcuts, don't mistake the effort of reading this for the real work.

Which is *writing*.

"Oh yeah," people say when I tell them what I do for a living, "I always meant to write a book." Damn near every jackass who was taught their ABCs in grade school thinks they can type the next Great Novel/Memoir/Navel-Gazing Guide/whatever. Just sit in a chair and type, it's simple, right?

Yeah. Just like vomiting. Very simple, but the trick is hitting the receptacle meant to flush it tidily away.

Most of it is simple ignorance—and the slew of "everyone can self-publish!" doesn't help dispel the myth that all you have to do is get drunk and spew words at whatever bowl is handy. Writing every day won't make you Shakespeare, just like practicing the piano won't make you Chopin. You will, however, end up the best piano player (or the most productive writer) around for more than a few country miles.

My advice, posted on my blog for years, is aimed at those who want to *make a living* writing. There are no guarantees, but producing a quality product over and over again will eventually find you an audience. Unfortunately, that's only the first step. After you've figured out how to produce quality writing, there's getting edited, following submission guidelines, contract negotiations (you should get an agent, as Caitlin Kittredge once memorably said, because you can literally lose count of how many ways there are to get screwed without one) and waiting to receive said contracts, copyediting, proofing, cover art, and once the damn thing is on the shelves, you're still not done. Because there's reviews and marketing to deal with, and in between all that, you still have to produce quality work.

You still have to sit down, over and over again, and do the work, even when sometimes you don't feel like it.

A writer *writes*. It's amazing how often this simple fact is overlooked. Plenty of people call themselves "writers" when they maybe open up the file—for the same (unfinished) book they've been working on for multiple years—every couple of months. Plenty of people who fritter away their energy on "building a platform" call themselves writers without producing jackshit. I could go on and on with the taxonomy of Speshul Snoflakes, but what would be the point?

A writer writes. Period.

A writer who *wants to improve* writes regularly. Getting into the habit of discipline is hard, falling out of it is easy. Writing every day for twenty minutes (or a set number of words) won't automatically get you published, but it will get you and your craft a lot closer to that goal.

I have been pilloried a few times for saying I believe a writer should write every day. Of course there will be days when you can't. Illness, accident, life all get in the way. Some professionals get by with long periods of inactivity, but they're exceptions rather than the rule. Good on them, but I'm not concerned with them. Yes, I think a writer should write every day. Period. No, I don't think I'm wrong. Yes, you're entitled to your own opinion. Have at it.

Some of my advice won't work for you. There are many different ways up the mountain, of course. These posts, usually sparked by questions from Readers or fellow writers, are just signposts. Your chances of getting up the damn mountain are a lot better if you know how someone else survived, and at least listen to how they got there.

Of course all this goes for getting published, too. There is a healthy dose of luck involved in getting published, be it with trad or small-press or what-have-you. The best you can do is produce a quality product and maximize your changes, so that sooner or later when Opportunity knocks, you can tear open the door, brain him, and drag him inside.

Chance favoring the prepared mind, and all that.

Lastly, there's a lot of self-publishing out there. There is very little quality control; consequently, most self-publishing is dreck. Getting a good editor, how to tell a good editor from a bad one, figuring out what quality control you need for your work, will maximize your chances of having a self-published book that actually *sells*.

There is no shortcut, there never was. All I can offer are these signposts, in the hope that they'll be useful.

The Use of Pain

January 5, 2006

I am in moderate pain from yesterday (which seems to have been the worst day yet in terms of stiffness pain from the accident in December) and I have pulled a few tails today, as well as unloaded the dishwasher. Now, after having taken my muscle relaxants, I am ready to wax pontifical.

I read a wonderful post about canon today by the fabulous Sarah Monette[1]. Any time I start hearing "canon" or "tradition" my hackles rise, my fascination with classical antiquity notwithstanding. Tradition and canon seem to me to be the best way to strangle new art, or truly socially-relevant art (think Sinclair's *The Jungle*). But then I have to yank myself up short and remind myself that it is merely my contrary streak speaking.

DH: You're a contrarian.

Me: (in injured tones) I am *not!*

To put my thinking concisely: if you read as well as write, you cannot hope but be influenced by the canon and the social/cultural atmosphere you're raised in/swimming in/living in. Canon exists to give us a point of reference, as the post on canon points out. Communities of people who read the same things and meet to hash out one point or another are as old as

---

[1] http://truepenny.livejournal.com Post is locked and unavailable.

civilization. (I'm sure there were poets in Sumerian times who got together to hash and cut. And what is religious epic poetry if not the earliest form of fanfic?)

All fiction is, to some degree or another, socially relevant; the very idea of fiction would be impossible without a social framework. A novel does not have to be very good to reveal the social underpinnings of the writer's viewpoint. We leave our fingerprints without ever guessing it. The novel cannot be divorced from the culture it is a product of.

This is why it is so important for writers to *read*. For God's sake, if you do not read you have no business writing. For one thing, reading will teach you what works on the page and what doesn't. It is the best way to learn nuance, tone, and pace—none of which can be taught in a class or workshop.

There is another purpose reading serves: it grounds you firmly in your own culture. I am not expressing this well. Let me use a metaphor. Listen closely. **Picasso could break the rules of art because he knew them thoroughly and had internalized them.** The post makes the valid point that "quality" literature has long been a province of dead white men. Unfortunately, they had the leisure and the resources to give to their Muse, while others were busy scrabbling for survival in one way or another. As Bukowski points out endlessly, a man writes much better on a full stomach than on an empty one, Rimbaud notwithstanding. And as soon as women fought for and received their educational rights—the ones lost largely when that crowd stoned Hypatia to death—they started producing fine writing.

I have a mental experiment I often use to illustrate a variant of this specific point. Imagine all the writing ever done, whether published or not. Now, imagine the proportion of each class/race/historical period's writing that is good and will endure. Imagine the vast mass of ephemera that will *not* endure. The proportion is about the same in any population, whether it's Dead White Male Writers or New Hot Minority Writers. The Dead White Male Writers had better press agents and more resources, ergo their quality writing has survived in greater proportion, just like the tombs of the Egyptian rich survived in greater proportion than the simple graves of the common folk.

Economic conditions dictated what percentage of writing would actually get written and what percentage of good writing from a certain population would endure. However, writing is not merely a product of economic conditions. I am fond of remarking that it is like a sickness, an obsession; even when I couldn't afford to write I somehow did because I could not imagine doing otherwise. But if I had not been a privileged member of a privileged class (a middle-class Caucasian woman in 20th-century America) I perhaps would have not had the opportunities I've had to get my voice heard. The internet is a great example of this: the great pluralization of information among anyone who can afford even a relatively cheap 486 and a modem. On one hand, the advent of relatively-cheap technology has made the explosion of minority literature possible to the greatest degree since Alexandria or even Moorish Spain.

To bring us back from this fascinating digression about economics, I will return to the beginning: canon exists to give us a frame of reference. One can't write a knock-off of Tolkien without reading him. (One can hardly write fantasy at all without reading Tolkien sooner or later, if only to make sure you're not unconsciously plagiarizing.) If one reads enough fantasy, one will end up at Tolkien's door just to find out what everyone else is talking about. This is culture at its finest, a commonly-agreed reference point that provides a measure for behavior. That the behavior is the abstract process of producing a fantasy novel does not detract from the practicality of having a canon.

Canons express the laws that, whether one likes them or not, must be at least looked at and internalized. Only then can they be broken in any meaningful way to produce—yes, you've got it, more canons. Humans are canon creatures: we like the comfort of habit and rules, sometimes to our own detriment. We also like to run up against the rules and change them—what else is fantasy *for*? Both urges, creation and destruction, are necessary for us to keep our balance and stay afloat in this sea we call culture.

Well, I have wound myself up in a ball of sentences and am not even sure if I've made sense. I'll leave that to the Reader to decide. Of course I've left out many important points when it comes to fiction. But I'm tired, and need more coffee, and to chew on this fascinating concept a little more.

When it comes right down to it, being a writer means chewing on interesting "what-ifs" and concepts the whole day long. And that, friends and neighbors, is the best work of all.

PS: I find it synchronous and wonderful that today's Word of the Day is *exegete*.

Trusting the Work

March 21, 2006

In my writing classes, I often focus on creative self-defense. No, it's not karate-chopping with a handful of dry pasta (though that can work). When I say "creative self-defense," I mean taking care of yourself so you can produce a work of art. It's a difficult thing to do.

First there's the brute work of typing sixty to a hundred thousand words. Then there's all the false starts, the sentences and scenes that go nowhere. There's the unruly characters and the merging plotlines, and having to trust it will all come out all right, that the little furled-tight space in your head where the butterfly lives will produce a coherent story. *Then* there's the revisions. Let's not even talk about those. Gargh.

I'm working on the fifth *Dante Valentine* book now. It's about forty thousand words along, and it's hard going. Part of it is that I hate to say goodbye to these characters and all they've meant to me, part of it is I hate putting them through what I'm going to have to do to them to make the story. Part of it is the nervousness every artist feels before a performance—a gymnast eyeing the parallel bars, for example, or a sprinter examining the racetrack, a rock star listening to the crowd bay after the opening act. This is when I feel the most acute performance anxiety. (There's another brand of anxiety right before a book release, but it's nothing compared to this torture.)

There's always a point, about a third of the way through a book, when it just seems so bloody fucking hopeless. *I can't do this*, I think. *I've bitten off more than I can chew. I cannot do this. There is no way I can possibly do this.* It isn't writer's block. I know what happens next and each sentence unreels smoothly in front of my fingers. It isn't even indecision—the river has no choice but to follow its banks, even if it floods. I know where the story goes. The trouble is, I doubt myself. Can I be clear enough? Can I pull off this twist in midair, can I stick this landing? Of course the readers expect a whopping good story, and my characters expect me to remain faithful to them (Hell hath no fury like a character forced to do something uncharacteristic) and my editor expects me not to mangle the Queen's English *too* badly.

But what I expect of myself is to be a channel for the story, to let it develop organically, to get myself out of the way and let it be. The acute attack of hopelessness yesterday is nothing new. I've suffered it with every book (except *Hunter's Prayer*). I was actually hyperventilating yesterday, looking at the situation I've gotten Dante into (room full of demons, one Hellesvront agent, and a seriously pissed-off lover—and this is after the imps and the Magi, and the swordfight on top the speeding antigrav tram) and thinking, *My God, I could have been a gynecologist. Or a lawyer.*

Of course, writing every day for a decade and a half will give you a number of strategies for dealing with this difficult time. Chief among them is the roaring drunk, but when you're looking after kids, that's not an option. It's also hard on the body when one is approaching thirty. Chocolate's good, but the amount of time one has to spend at the treadmill after inhaling a quarter-tonne is daunting to say the least.

Actually, I did hit the treadmill with some good music. I turned the whole mess over to the characters. In essence, I told 'em: "You figure this thing out. When you're ready I'll come back. Fight somewhere I can't hear you, and I'm going to trust this will all come out all right." Of course Dante's reply was unprintable, as she stamped away flicking a knife around her fingers. The sudden sense of peace was overwhelming. My God, but that woman is high-maintenance.

Physical exercise is one of the best ways to deal with this kind of nervousness, but there's also a component of trust. After twenty-two novels written (some of which will never see the light of day; only five are published now and another one's due out in September) I think I have finally begun to relax a little when I hit this point. A very, very little.

My point, which I am wending toward with many side-trips, is this: **trust the work**. Stories don't come through for no reason. Each teaches you something, even the unfinished ones. Characters mutate, slide into finished works, plot aspects and arcs merge, each story is a laboratory of effects and shadows. Let them be.

Trust the work—and not so incidentally, trust yourself. It's a leap of faith like any creative work. We fling ourselves out into space again and again, and each time the net catches us in one way or another. The most terrifying moment is not when we're contemplating the jump, but after we've thrown ourselves off the platform of the safe and the known and are tumbling in freefall, writing the story, letting the words and the characters do what they want and scrambling to keep up. There is the point of no return, when we have to trust the air itself will carry us and we will alight at that place at the end of the story, where the characters smile or weep, and bid farewell for a short while or forever. Remember that scene in *Ghost* where the spirits are lined up outside Whoopi Goldberg's door, each one waiting patiently for its turn to slide in and tell its story? Think of it that way.

I promise you there are always more stories, and they have chosen you—just you—for a reason. Whether you paint, or sing, or draw, or run, or build cars, or fix dishwashers, you're performing art. That art has chosen you because you are the person who can do it the way it wants to be done.

If you can't trust yourself, trust the stories. They know what they're doing.

Of course, the roaring drunk and the quarter-tonne of chocolate are always options, as are window-shopping and turning up some reprehensible music and flinging yourself around your living room in a facsimile of dancing (another one of my favorites). Use with care—just because they're options doesn't mean you HAVE to use them.

But that's another story.

On FanFic

March 22, 2006

It's a subject that manages to divide writers, especially published writers, and I'm going to say it a few times so we all get over the shock of hearing a "dirty word." Fanfic. Fanfic. Fanfic. Are you hyperventilating yet?

whitemunin[2] on LiveJournal mentioned offhand in an email the other day that she'd developed a thick hide after dealing with insta-reviews in the world of fanfic. This is a good thing, and I'm about to tell you why—and I'm about to tell you why writing fanfic is even necessary. Are you ready?

A lot of people knock fanfic, saying it detracts from the author's royalty statements and infringes on the author's copyrights. Personal opinion: as long as the people doing the fanfic aren't getting paid for it, I think it's fine. It only takes reading a few fanfics to be curious about the stories that originally engendered the fanfic; and by and large fanfic authors are rabid fans who buy every book of their Favorite Author's as soon as it hits the shelves in hardback. Frankly, I don't see where all this free publicity is a bad thing. Stories are a dime a dozen, they're lined up out the damn door, and if someone uses my characters in slash or just plain fic I'm more inclined to see it as 1. free

---

[2] http://whitemunin.livejournal.com Post locked and unavailable.

marketing I don't have to sweat over, and 2. the sincerest form of flattery.

That's not the point of this post, though. Fanfic is a phase every damn writer goes through. It's necessary. Imitation is how human beings *learn*, and there is no better way to learn characterization, tone, voice, and pacing than by following someone's example, as long as that someone's voice resonates for you. It's just like training wheels for a writer.

Let me clue you in on my own dirty little secret: I made a lot of my chops by writing horrid, torrid X-Men fanfic in my school notebooks. I never showed anyone those stories, and this was before the internet (gasp in wonder, my friends. Yes, I am *that* old). I learned what worked and what didn't on the page by mixing up the X-Men characters, adding a few of my own, and dreaming up storylines. It helped that during this time Claremont was writing and Lee drawing some of the best damn comic-book story and art I've ever seen. (If one has to imitate, imitate only the best.) It taught me a lot, and eventually I was hungry for...more. I wanted my own stories. I wanted to burst out of the confinement of someone else's universe and create my own. A Promethean urge, to be true, and one every writer should experience at one point or another. It was time to move on, and I did—but those lessons stayed with me. Boy howdy, did they ever stay with me.

In other words, I shamelessly aped and imitated until I learned to ride the bike on my own, and then I was off and wheeling down the path, unable to stop even if I'd tried.

The problem comes when fanfic writers feel the need to burst the boundaries to write something of their own and *don't*, whether out of fear or for another reason. Then the training wheels become chains, and nitpicking over canon (we all know who these writers are) turns into bitterness and fascist picking at other artists. Sadly, often these writers don't even know they're bitter and trammeled, and trying to tell them only engages the defensive reflex. On the other hand, those who surmount this hurdle are usually much more in tune with their own creative health.

The other big problem with fanfic is feedback. More precisely, it's taking feedback personally. It is an amazement and wonder to me that fanfic writers get personal over characters not "theirs" to begin with. And God forbid you mention to some fanficcers little points of craft like, say, grammar. And spelling. Of course, when the characters are your own (sometimes even when they're not) and you've poured your heart and soul into the damn manuscript, it's difficult to take even the gentlest constructive criticism gratefully. When you add in the Bitter FanFiccers out to hurt anyone they can to salve their own pain, you have an explosive combination.

Here's the trick: **only read feedback once a week.**

Really. Read that again. Only. Read. Feedback. Once. A. Week. Not only does that give you a block of time to sit down and get it all over with, but it will help you make sure the majority of your time is devoted to—you guessed it—writing instead of getting into petty little battles over whether or not your fic follows someone's ideas of canon. It also makes it easier to tear away once you hit the point of taking the training wheels off.

Here's another little tip: if one person says it, it's opinion. If two people say it, coincidence. If three people mention the same thing about your story or your writing, it has got to change. (Unless it is a positive something, in which case cherish it.) That's my particular Rule of Three, and it works very well.

The fact remains, there will always be people who hate what you write, for whatever reason. They may think they hate you. So be it. One's job as a writer is to tell the truth using fiction, and that enrages some people, especially when it's done well. Someone may not agree with your worldview. So what? The world is wide and opinions and worldviews are like rectums: everyone's got one. The trick is to find your audience, the people who *do* like what you write, and write coherently and well enough that THEY have a good time.

We are communicators, us writers, and that's our job. Feedback is valuable inasmuch as it tells us whether we're communicating clearly ENOUGH. But don't fall into the trap of thinking the feedback is a comment on you. Lots of feedback—especially the obviously nasty personal kind—reflects more on the person *giving* than the person receiving. Remember this, and stay gracious.

Above all, consider it practice for being edited. Being edited hurts. There is no way around it. As Westley says, "Life is pain. Anyone who tells you otherwise is selling something."

It is going to hurt no matter what, because what you write feels pretty damn personal to you. It is your baby, your darling, you sweat over its birth and its first steps, you are intimately involved with making it at every step. Getting feedback, getting reviews, getting edited HURTS. Okay, it hurts like hell. Like fiery, aching, tormenting, Inferno-esque, Middle-Ages Inquisition HELL. Get over it. There is pain in every area of human endeavor. Our job is to write through the pain and learn from it, not to moan or get bitter because it hurts. 'Nuff said.

Those fanficcers who manage to avoid these dual traps often go on to produce wonderful work. Sadly, they are a small proportion, which is not a surprise when you think of how many "writers" there are out there "don't have time" to write. (That's a whole 'nother rant.)

If you do write fanfic, be aware it's a valuable phase but not the end-all and be-all of the writing life. Also be aware that feedback is a double-edged sword, like most things in life. But above all, understand you cannot afford to remain still. It's called inspiration for a reason, it moves and breathes. Staying in one place for too long can suffocate.

Last but not least, if you're getting paid for soaking off another person's character and universe, be aware it's not fanfic. It's plagiarism. There's a special circle of Hell, worse even than editing, reserved for that. End of story.

Fame and Women

April 27, 2006

I have my favorite heroines, both historical and fictional.

On the historical end there's Athenais de Montespan, Cleopatra, Medea (especially when a woman writes her, like in the *Virago Book of Evil Women*; yes, I know she's not strictly historical but I classify her there), and for sheer ballsiness, Eleanor Roosevelt, Mother Jones and female Russian and Finnish snipers in World War II. There's also Zenobia and the Empress Theodora (*The purple is the noblest winding-sheet*), not to mention Sacajawea (she did everything *they* did, only carrying a baby and saving their silly butts as well). And Maid Marian, though I don't know if she qualifies as historical either.

Still, it's to literary and movie heroines my heart belongs. I love heroical historical maidens, but still I am depending on historians to tell me what they thought and felt. I can imagine, and letters and personal papers make it easier, but still—who really bares their soul in a letter? Even Heloise's or the Portuguese Nun's letters have that veneer of artifice any letter acquires. But a novel or movie heroine is laid open for me to see, and I like that. So here we are, at my literary and movie heroines.

No list of my literary heroines would be complete without Tanith Lee. My favorites are the narrator of *The*

Birthgrave and Rachaela from the *Scarabae Blood Opera* series, though Rach is so passive and vituperative as to make my teeth grit. (I also conflate Rachaela with Smilla Jaspersen, more about her below.) Also Esther from *Days of Grass* should get a nod here. But when it comes to creating a heroine, my first and best love goes to Tanith Lee.

What do I look for in a literary heroine? First I look for a writer who has enough craft to write a woman. We are not so easily written, we with ovaries. Men have the benefit of two thousand years of driving us out of public discourse and taking up all the space on the page, and a man's motivations have already been thoroughly covered from Suetonious and Ovid onward. I'm not saying they don't have depths, I'm just saying...well, whenever a man's written, I usually have the feeling I've seen it before. Maybe that's just my cynicism. But a woman...she is a different tale. Even female authors have trouble crafting a woman who can stand up on the written page, because we are writing through a lattice of male perceptions and conventions when it comes to women. I cannot count how many female authors I've read who have women behaving like a bad SNL skit of what a man thinks a woman is.

Enough of that tangent. The first thing I look for is a writer who can write a woman.

Next, I look for a list of qualities. Is the character internally consistent? Does she have a fatal flaw? Does she act instead of react, and if she reacts is it clear to me *why*? Is she strong without being a Mary Sue? Is she capable of eating her own heart? Is she multifaceted, capable of strength and gentleness? If she is *not* capable of gentleness, you'd better show me why, buddy. This is why Lee gets first place. Her women breathe, and even if I don't agree with their motivations I still *understand* them. Dorothy Allison's Bone gets second, even though *Bastard Out Of Carolina* makes me cry.

What other heroines do I adore? Smilla. Smilla! From *Smilla's Sense of Snow*, which is written so beautifully I rationed the pages as I got closer to the end. From the very first chapter this damaged, brilliant, and stubborn woman had me. This book is one of the few I buy multiple copies of so we can give away. Smilla never looks back once she's taken her sword from the sheath, she merely plunges ahead to find the truth. I appreciate that in a heroine.

Next up is Teresa in Arturo Perez-Reverte's *The Queen of the South*. We all know about my fetish for Perez-Reverte. But he actually managed to *write* a woman, and he did it so beautifully I had to gasp for breath several times. What discussion of literary heroines would be complete without Shakespeare? There's Lady Macbeth, of course, who had bigger balls than her husband. And there's Portia, who argues for her beloved's life as a cross-dressing lawyer. Of course, the great Will was trammeled by the view of women in his society, but under Queen Elizabeth's influence he produced some mighty fine female characters.

Who else? There is Lolita, of course, who struggles desperately to free herself from a pedophile's solipsism. There is Robin McKinley's Beauty and Deerskin, though Deerskin wins for sheer aching courage. There is Steven Brust's Tazendra, always ready for a fight. There are Shkai'ra and Megan from SM Stirling and Shirley Meier. There is Sarah Dessen's Caitlin and Cynthia Voight's Dicey, as well as Hermione Granger. Not to mention Peter Beagle's Last Unicorn, who committed the brave act of not falling into a stupid happy ending that would rob her of self-respect.

That's another thing about literary heroines. The heroine who stops short of the self-fulfillment she has fought for during most of the book drives me to fits of rage. I realize this is a convention, but I will die and go to hell before I let a character of mine do so—unless it's necessary to the story. But so often the HEA is a copout, a writer gets to within forty pages of the end and introduces a *deus ex machina* to suck all the life and wonder out of a female protagonist. This is most marked in movies. There are very few movies in American cinema where a woman who has control of her own sexuality isn't mutilated in one way or another by the end of the film, made to "pay" for the grievous sin of being female and sleeping with whoever she deems fit.

For this reason one of my favorite film heroines is Bridget from *The Last Seduction*, who manipulates her way through a web of sex, lies, theft, adultery, betrayal, and murder—and she comes out on top. She *wins*, and it's so delicious. I also love the Papist spy-prostitute in *Brotherhood of the Wolf*. And who could forget Angelina Jolie's Gia or Bonnie? (Cornell Woolrich wrote the novella *Original Sin* is based on, it's titled *Waltz Into Darkness* and the woman gets away with it there too.) Then there's Linda Hamilton in the *Terminator* movies and Peta Wilson in the *Nikita* series, both strong kickass women. (Yes, I know the original Nikita is better. Shut up.) There's something about a girl with a gun and a mission, trying to keep her own soul in the middle of slaughter, that appeals to me. Beatrix Kiddo from *Kill Bill* also deserves a mention here, since I watched the first *Kill Bill* over and over again as I wrote no few of the Danny Valentine books. I do occasionally like the more traditional heroines too. I love Myrna Loy as Nora in the *Thin Man* series. Julie in Kieslowski's *Bleu* also holds a special place in my heart for sheer vulnerable strength. Stephen King's Beverly Marsh (back to books) deserves an honorable mention, as does Ivy Walker in *The Village*. There's no shortage of women to love in fiction and on the silver screen.

Still, that's enough for now. You get the idea. Who are your favorite fictional women? Don't worry, the heroes will have their day. But today, it's all about the girls.

Fasten Your Seatbelts, Boys

May 6, 2006

After my recent ode to heroines, I thought it only fair to give the guys a little room. Heaven knows I'm hard on my heroes, in more ways than one. I expect Very Great Things from them, and abuse them at every opportunity. As I've said before, men have been hogging the public stage for the past two thousand years. I consider their motivations at least well, if not thoroughly, plumbed. (No offense, guys. But you *have* been a mite loud.) So who are my favorite heroes?

Let's start with a brief recap of my favorite historical figures: Leonidas, who kicked ass and died well at Thermopylae; Cicero and Ovid could between them talk a girl into anything, and who could forget Hannibal? (The general, not the cannibal.) I am more than fond of Gibbon in my own quiet way, and am fascinated by Louis de Saint-Just, Danton, Robespierre, and Camille Desmoulins as both heroes and antiheroes. Talleyrand and Napoleon both qualify as heroes to me. In modern times I am fascinated by Churchill and Noam Chomsky, both extremely intellectually attractive. Though I will confess to having a morbid need to ruffle Chomsky's hair and call him a button. And let's not even get started about my shameful lust for Jon Stewart and Stephen Colbert. But let's get to the meat of it, shall we? Let's turn to heroes both literary and film.

Oddly enough, while Jane Eyre falls more into my historical female category, Mr. Rochester makes it into my literary heroes list. He just seems a little less real than Jane does to me, though he is a nice change from all the pretty-boy heroes we're used to. Van in Nabokov's *Ada* seems more real, strangely. To round out the trifecta, there's Tanith Lee's Cyrion, who is the thinking woman's Conan. No barbarians for me, thank you. Lee does give the best heroes to match her heroines. Verlis in *Metallic Love* is stunning, as well as Jace in *Sometimes, After Sunset*. There's Daniel Vehmund in *Heart-beast*, Azhrarn in *Tales from the Flat Earth*, and Althene in the *Blood Opera* books. (Heroine? Hero? I'm putting her in hero category.)

Azhrarn is probably the best instance of an ambiguous hero. We shouldn't find him so attractive—he is, after all, a sociopath—but by the end of the books we are...well, we root for him, don't we? I do. Try as I might to like alpha males, the fact remains I usually go for beta heroes, like Jet in *Resurrection Man* or Kit in Diane Duane's *Wizard* series. I am passing fond of the Beast in McKinley's *Beauty*, and my own retellings of *Beauty and the Beast* is informed by that book in more ways than one. There's Joscelin in the Kushiel books, who plays second fiddle to Phedre but is still a hero in his own right, and whose pain informs the trilogy in startling ways. Who can forget Westley, from *The Princess Bride*, played so swimmingly by Cary Elwes? But more about movie heroes in a minute.

Other literary heroes I adore are: John Constantine (from the *Hellblazer* comics, thank you, not Keanu Reeves), William of Baskerville from Eco's *The Name of the Rose*, and Cat in Joan Vinge's *Psion* books.

What do these disparate heroes all share? Courage goes without saying, and self-sacrifice. I love me a self-sacrificin' hero. But I don't like a man who just throws himself into the sacrificing. There has to be a little dithering. There has to be redemption—lots of redemption—and a hint of danger to the man himself. Like, "I could kill you. There's always that choice. I *choose* to be a good boy...but I could so easily go wrong." Which is why I like beta heroes so much, I think. I like that edge of a man who can go to the dark side if he needs to, and not a lot of authors have the *cojones* to give us a nasty hero. (Shut up about Thomas Covenant. He doesn't count.) I like redemptive heroes in particular, men who find something to fight for, something *worth* fighting for. Or heroes like Cat, who are shoved into no-win situations and stick to their personal codes, despite the cost.

Let's not forget Don Simon Ysidro, who I was introduced to through my friend Jan. Every once in a while we both blink and sigh, "Don *Siiiiiiimon*," and forget he's a nasty murdering vampire. For this reason, my favorite literary hero is Ged the wizard in the *Earthsea* trilogy—but not in the third book. Rather, I like the Ged of the first and second books, especially the *Tombs of Atuan*. Ged as a character really needs someone else—like his shadow, or Tenar—to play off before he becomes real and three-dimensional. Still, his fierceness, and the fact that he doesn't always win without a terrible cost, are fascinating. He's easily one of the most complex male personalities in fantasy literature.

Let's go on to movies, shall we? In particular, *The Princess Bride* is chock-full of marvelous heroes. Westley is given a good run for his money by Inigo Montoya (oh, Mandy Patinkin, how we love thee), and even Count Rugen and the Sicilian qualify as zany heroes in their own right. Then there's Viggo Mortensen's Aragorn. (Yes, you knew I was going to go there. Shut up.) Mortensen's great strength is he played Aragorn quieter and quieter except for bursts of frustration, bypassing Tolkien's sudden torrent of thees and thous in Aragorn's speech during *Return of the King*.

Matt Damon in the *Bourne* movies deserves a mention here. He could have so easily fallen into bathos, but he didn't. He played Bourne dirty and conflicted, and I like that. There's Bruce Campbell's Ash and Elvis, both fantastic and funny little men. (Hail to the King, baby.) The gay homicide detective in *Boondock Saints* (played with such gusto by Willem Dafoe) is another of my favorites. Another is Joaquin Phoenix's Lucius Hunt in *The Village*, one of my favorite movies. Karol Karol in Kieslowski's *Blanc* deserves mention here, if only for his single-minded determination to get revenge, miscarrying at the last moment. Then there's Al Pacino's Johnny in *Frankie and Johnny*, who is just the kind of mad weirdo who would fall in love with me. Minus the felony part, that is.

Last but not least, there is the entire cast of *Dead Poets Society*, all heroes in their own little ways (except for that redheaded kid. Him, we can shoot. In the movie, I mean). DPS *is* my favorite movie, if only because it encompasses so much—literature, art, life, love, conformity, the perils of unorthodoxy, the power of words to soothe or enrage...and I cry every single time I see it. Seriously. Sobbing. In front of the TV, on my knees, *sobbing*. Man, I love that movie.

There are classic movie heroes—Bogart in *Casablanca*, Tom Hardy in that one *Wuthering Heights*, Jimmy Stewart and John Wayne in *The Man Who Shot Liberty Valance*, Bogart again in *The Big Sleep*—and the über ultra, Marlon Brando in *On the Waterfront*. He plays Terry Malloy with such dimwitted tenderness and sheer stubborn violence it's hard not to fall for him. I failed miserably. I still watch that movie about once a month, and I enjoy it every time. Yum.

I've just noticed none of my heroes are musclebound. Huh. Of course, most of them are plenty dangerous if they're crossed, but none of them are Arnold

Lilith Saintcrow

Schwarzenegger-ripped. I did always tend to go for the rapier-lean quicklings anyway.

There it is, my heroes list. I'm sure there are ones I've forgotten...so tell me, who are yours?

The Right Ending

May 22, 2006

Alot of you have written to take me to task, dear Readers, and I think it's time I explained myself. It will save us both so much grief, and I hope you will understand a little better after I tell you what I'm about to tell you.

I do not believe in happy endings. I believe in the *right* ending.

I don't have anything against happy endings. I really don't. What I hate, what I loathe utterly with every ounce of my being, is when a writer or filmmaker betrays the *right* ending of a piece because they want a *happy* ending. They build this edifice of bittersweet wonder, and sell it for a cheap Hallmark card tacked on the end. It's maddening. Not every story ends happily, and we shouldn't want them to.

Fellini refused to put happy endings on his movies, because then people wouldn't go home and change their lives. I refuse to shoehorn a happy ending onto a book because it is my job, dear Reader, to tell you the truth through the lattices of story. Often, out here in the real world, the endings are unsatisfactory at best and downright nasty at worst. I would be lying to you if I created a gritty, pulpy world with a flawed heroine and a dangerous cast of characters, and had everything turn into a bloody Barneythe-dinosaur singalong at the end. I would be *failing* you. I refuse to do that. If I am going to tell you a story, I am going to make it as true as I can, the type of truth that resonates.

As *V* says: "Artists tell lies to tell the truth, politicians tell lies to cover the truth up." I am not a politician.

I can hear the whining already. *But Lili! We read stories to escape!*

No you don't.

You read stories because it is a human hunger to communicate, because it is a human hunger to tell and retell and listen to stories. We make the world, our world, through the stories we tell ourselves.

To draw a metaphor, we don't eat because we like Twinkies. We eat because we are hungry and must nourish ourselves. It's okay if you don't like the endings. Really, it is. It doesn't hurt my feelings. On the contrary, it heartens me.

For example, when you write to me telling me you cried for Danny Valentine, that it wasn't fair, and that you felt for her so deeply you could really hate me for giving that ending to her first book...well, I don't exactly dance with glee, but I do feel satisfied. Because I've given you the best story I can, with the truest beginning and ending I can, with the truest characters I can. You are responding to that truth when you cry for her, or when you get angry at me on her behalf. She has become a real, living person to you. How could I be angry or discouraged by that?

I am not saying I don't write happy endings. I do. When they are true. Like *Hunter, Healer*, for example. That ending came as a result of a lot of struggle and sacrifice, at a terrible cost for both main characters. It was happy, but it was also true, as true as I could make it. How about *Dark Watcher*? Again, a terrible amount of struggle and sacrifice, and a terrific cost—but the ending satisfied, did it not? In *Working for the Devil*, the ending was bittersweet at best. But

I don't call it a sad ending by any means. Dante got what she wanted: revenge. She also got something infinitely more precious: the ability to become vulnerable again, to care. If Jace had showed up at her door again before Lucifer's agent had, do you think the Dante at the beginning of the book would have let him stay? Do you think she would have bent enough to admit she needed someone there? It's not a perfect ending, but it was the only ending the book could have. Because it was true.

I make a promise each time I write for you, dear Reader, that I will tell the truth as best I can, happy ending or not. After all, there is a great deal more hope in a **true** ending than there is in a **happy** one. I'm always a sucker for hope.

Where Do They Come From?

June 8, 2006

Where do you get your ideas? Of all the questions a writer dreads, this is one of the worst. Because, well, most writers don't know. Ideas come from that far country presided over by our sylphlike and aggressive (and sometimes downright bitchy) Muses, who are, let there be no doubt, female. They are deep and full of passion, and willing to spill their secrets to the right listener—but they do expect to be petted, listened to, and occasionally courted. They do need pretty gifts and interesting bits of things. Hell hath no fury like a Muse scorned. Oh, she will kick your ass. Will she ever.

My favorite answer to "Where do you get your ideas?" actually comes from Stephen King, who replied tongue-in-cheek, "The Idea-of-the-Month Club, of course. You get your featured idea and two alternates mailed monthly." He did go on to remark that even he doesn't know.

Getting an idea is like being hit in the head with a padded hammer. Yes, it's padded. But sheezus, it's still a bloody hammer. Sometimes a character will start whispering in my ear, and I'll have to take dictation or they won't leave me alone. Other times I see a scene—an action, or just a shot like a film clip, replaying over and over in stunning detail. I will have to write to find out what's going on, who the characters are, and how this thing ends up.

Usually seeing a scene or hearing a character whisper is just the beginning of a long three-month race to the finish line that plumbs the depths of my strength and drains me of all other thought and emotion while I feverishly type to get the book out of my head so I can sleep and eat again. I am literally possessed by books once they heat up. Family have learned to recognize the signs—muttering to myself, staring off into the distance at dinner, distracted even when it comes to washing dishes, suddenly breaking off in the middle of conversations to block a scene out inside my head.

I've learned to get out of the driver's seat and let the Muse have her way, which isn't as easy as it sounds. All my usable RAM gets taken up with writing the book and keeping the plot lines going, with none left over for little things like eating or navigating. The only thing as important as the Muse, once a book heats up, is feeding the little people in the house. My daughter has even greeted visitors at the door with a cheerful, "Mommy's writing again, so you'll have to talk to me." (That is, visitors we know. Not the UPS man, who probably thinks I'm either a moron or hopelessly eccentric. Even I can't decide.) I've found that going out dancing, or to the track, helps me keep a tenuous connection to myself while the Muse is in the driver's seat. Physical activity that leaves me wrung-out can sometimes buy me a few hours' worth of sleep. Also, getting out of the house to work at the bookstore helps. If I'm exhausted by the end of the day it's easier to get some rest, or just go back and fine-tune previous scenes. Sometimes, and only sometimes, a little bit of wine will help. But I don't recommend that, because the social vision of the alcoholic writer is so strong.

But *where* do the bloody things come from? Ideas, that is.

I don't know. But I do know this: you have to feed your Muse before she starts hitting you with ideas.

Writers are intellectual magpies. We're always picking up bits of shiny concepts and ideas and consigning them to a mental slush pile. Occasionally something will spring rank, foul, and fast-growing from that compost. Voila! It's an idea, usually a very good one, nourished by several streams, myths, concepts, other books, movies, life experiences—a whole range of nutritious things that make your head full and your Muse happy. She will pick light-fingered through the rubbish bin, wave her hands, and magically hand you a piece of fine elvish jewelry that it's up to you to polish and bring out the best in. Before you know it, you have a book.

BUT, and this is a very big BUT, you **MUST FEED YOUR MUSE**.

There is no alternative. You must constantly stuff your head with new and interesting things. You must daydream, and look at pretty things, and find out what fires your particular Muse up and gets her going. You've got to throw an awful lot of stuff in the slush heap before it can start producing those pumpkins the size of wagon wheels.

In the end, it doesn't matter where the ideas come from. What matters is you keep yourself open and clear enough—and with a head full of interesting dreams enough—to catch them, and disciplined enough to follow them wherever they lead. It's hard work. But it's good work, if you can get it.

It's Official.
I've Died and Gone to Heaven

June 19, 2006

For the rest of my life, I will remember this past weekend. I should have left Friday night, I would have missed traffic. Saturday was a perfect storm of traffic conditions—the Fremont fair, the art-car rally, a Mariners game, and the Gay Pride Parade as well as the Locus events. I got caught in various versions of stop-and-go from Fort Lewis all the way up to Seattle, yo. Still, there were no accidents, and I arrived at the hotel more or less in one piece, stopping only to check in and wash my face before heading out to the autograph party for the Locus awards.

When I got to the EMP (Experience Music Project building, for those of you who haven't lived in Seattle) I found out two things: 1. There is a science fiction museum in the EMP building. 2. Lea Day rocks, for I popped into the autograph room to tell her I'd shown up (finally) and said I was going to go get myself a badge so I didn't get thrown out. Immediately she grinned, and I knew what she was going to say. *"Batches? We doan need no stinking batches!"* she cried. It just got better from there.

Dear Readers, I was taken behind the autograph table to meet Anne McCaffrey, her son Todd McCaffrey, and Elizabeth Ann Scarborough. With stars in my eyes I immediately started babbling. I'm surprised none of them took a tranquilizer gun to me. Anne was busy signing, but she graciously accepted the copy of *Fire Watcher* I brought for her (she has the rest of the Watcher books) and greeted me warmly. Todd and Annie (Ms. Scarborough) greeted me just as warmly and made me feel at home, despite being busy signing as well. It's so good to be among writers. When I said, "My head feels like a piece has been ripped out—I did 7K on the Valentine book yesterday," (which I did, BTW) they all immediately understood I was enduring a case of birth pangs, and reassured me it would be all right with enough whiskey and a good dose of hanging-out.

Neil Gaiman was at the signing party, and as he left I had a chance to catch his eye (by planting myself firmly in his path like the little fangirl I am). I managed to gasp out, "Big fan...love your work..." and he graciously nodded and thanked me. He was on his way to the Locus awards proper, so there was no slowing down or stopping (or maybe I had a look in my eye like I was going to grab him and start talking at a million miles an hour. I think I could have restrained myself...but it's probably for the best) but still: *I was in the same room with Anne McCaffrey and Neil Gaiman at the same time.* My jaw is still dropped. I was taken down the autograph table after that by Lea, and nearly frocking swooned when she announced, as I was shaking a particular gentleman's hand, "Lili Saintcrow, this is Greg Bear." I immediately started to gasp. "Warn me before you do that, Lea!" And there was much laughter. Lea introduced me around, and I saw Duane Wilkins from the University Bookstore, who is an absolute darling of a man. He recognized me from my own signing and we traded huge grins and wisecracks.

Then it was time to pop back to the hotel, both so Anne could rest and to get ready for the Hall of Fame event, which is what I ended up attending instead of the awards. I helped out as much as I could, and I think I was calm enough to do a good job. Back at the hotel, I had dinner with Tania Opland and Mike Freeman (who did the Masterharper CD, Mike is hilarious in his dry British way and Tania is a classy, wonderful lady); Lea, who is an ABSOLUTE DARLING; Annie Scarborough (who is so warm, funny, welcoming, and nice I was immediately put at ease); and a wonderful jeweler from the Peninsula and his lovely wife (Rick: Thank you for dinner. And I adore especially your scarab rings.). Monkeygirl popped by the table and sat next to me, and we immediately started bonding. Then it was time to go dress for the Hall of Fame ceremony.

Readers, I am an idiot. I didn't bring a single stich of anything that wasn't jeans or sleeping togs. Those of you who know me, know I am allergic to dresses—but I still would have worn one if I'd brought it. As it was, I had to make up for my lack of finery with loud jewelry, which I was adequately prepared to do. *grin* Monkeygirl and I bonded further over music and nail polish, and by the time we popped back down to the lobby to meet up with everyone and get ready to troop out the door, we were buds. After all, it's not every day you find someone who can immediately start finishing your sentences and gets all your song references—*and* Rocky Horror callback references.

The event was the induction of Frank Kelly Freas, Frank Herbert, George Lucas, and Anne McCaffrey into the Science Fiction Hall of Fame. Neil Gaiman was Master of Ceremonies, one more reason for me to stand in slackjawed awe of him. (Did you know he has twenty-six Locus awards now? But who's counting?)

Gaiman's opening speech is something I will never forget. He spoke about the power of the imagination, and how writers tend to downplay that power. After all, we're only doing what we love, as best as we know how. But as he pointed out (or as he told the story, as Alan Moore pointed out to him) everything we see that isn't a tree, rock, plant, or animal, someone had to imagine. Someone had to *create*. His words about never doubting that when we write we are engaged in nothing less than a magical act... I'm sorry. I'm tearing up as I type. It was a helluva speech, and such a vindication for me personally to hear. I keep forgetting, you see, that writing is an act of sorcery in the oldest and truest sense.

Plus, when he remarked he would give up breathing and sleeping for reading, if he could, I was nodding in agreement—and *so was everyone else in the room*. Which just about blew my mind.

The presentations were wonderful. Freas and Herbert have both passed on, but family members accepted the awards on their behalf. (I actually got to meet Brian Herbert, who is a stellar guy and was very kind to me.) George Lucas couldn't make it, but Rob Coleman accepted on his behalf. Right after Coleman did so, the 501st Stormtrooper Legion (affectionately known as Vader's Fist) took over the stage and presented Rob with honorary membership. It was one of the coolest moments of my life, to see stormtroopers, Boba Fett, Jedi, a Queen Amidala, and I think I saw a Sith Lord (but I'm not sure) standing on a stage.

Afterward, Neil Gaiman took the mike back. "God, I love this job," he said. Then Anne was inducted. We gave her a standing ovation, and I was proud as punch to be in the same room. Annie Scarborough's speech presenting her was beautiful. I about clapped my hands sore. After the ceremony we took a quick spin through the sci-fi museum itself. (Which is worth it, if only for the huge Aliens replica.)

Dear Readers, I stood in front of a case containing a first-edition of *Dragonflight*. And *Anne McCaffrey was right next to me*. I knelt down (she was sitting) and thanked her for writing. Let me take a small digression here.

The first time I opened *Dragonflight* I was in a junior-high school library. I can remember the carpeting and the tables, the entire room, and where I was sitting when I started in on that most fantastic of voyages—with Lessa, a heroine who was strong, fearless, unpredictable, and tender once her loyalty was won. In the years that followed I read all the McCaffrey I could find, and have read to pieces (literal falling-apart pieces) two copies of *To Ride Pegasus* and one of *Restoree*. Every time I opened a McCaffrey book, I knew I was going to find real characters and good writing. I started attempting book-length fantasy *because* of Anne McCaffrey.

I found other authors after I found her, but had I not stumbled across *Dragonflight* I don't know what would have become of me. *To Ride Pegasus* got me through any number of horrible experiences. To be standing next to her, and to be able to tell her, "Thank you so much for writing. I wouldn't be writing what I am if it wasn't for you." was magical. It was even more magical when she patted my hand and said, "My dear, thank God you're writing." For the rest of my life I will be proud of and unendingly grateful for that moment. It is one of the best gifts a writer can give, especially a writer whose work has been so genre-defining, to take the time to encourage a novice.

Writing is such a solitary art, and it's so fraught with self-doubt. A few words of encouragement and support can work wonders. Literally, for the rest of my life, I will never again be able to think of that moment without pushing back both tears and a deep feeling of gratefulness and utter, sheer, complete and total happiness in my life's work, what I've chosen to do as long as I have breath. Those six little words, taking no more than a few seconds, meant so much to me.

I never *dreamed*, when I started stumbling into the wilds of plot and character, that I would ever have the opportunity to do something like this.

We went back to the hotel, and gathered downstairs in the lounge. There was laughter and merriment, and congratulations to the new Hall of Famer. People drifted away and went to bed, a few more people came down, and I got sloshed and closed down the bar with the posse, including Lea, Monkeygirl, Todd McCaffrey, Mike Whelan, and other wonderful people I won't bore everyone with listing like a star-struck goober. I actually got to talk Latin grammar with Todd, too. When Mike Whelan arrived in a black leather jacket and shades, I opened my mouth and cried, "Neil!" with everyone else, and collapsed into laughter. It was four AM before I walked Lea to her room (Monkeygirl, poor thing, had to leave to go to work) and wended my still-very-very-tipsy way back to my room, to collapse in bed and think with amazement, my God. My God. Wow.

I slept a little, then got up the next morning and had to rush to make brunch with my youngest sister, who lives out in the U District of Seattle. I wasn't able to see everyone off, but I had made my goodbyes the night before. (Let me tell you: Mexican is the best hangover food. *Arroz con pollo* with a lot of water and a little ibuprofen will get you through almost any hangover.)

After that, we stopped in the University Bookstore, where I scored a new book on the French Revolution and bought my sis a copy of *Invitation to a Beheading*, my most recent you-must-read-this book. Then I had to start for home.

I was exhausted, and I ran into some bad traffic at Southcenter. (Took me an hour to go six miles.) But afterward it was smooth sailing, and I got home to greet the kidlings with squeals of delight. Total physical time spent: 48 hours. It was the experience of a lifetime. I will always remember sliding through downtown Seattle in Monkeygirl's car, listening to New Order.

I will always remember seeing everyone in the room nod in agreement that reading is just as essential as breath or sleep. I will always remember standing and clapping until my hands hurt for Anne. I will always remember "Batches? We doan need no stinking batches!"

In closing...thank you. Thanks are due to Lea, who has been my fairy godmother in this strange new world; to Anne for being so wonderfully gracious; to Annie Scarborough for making me feel at home; to Todd for the encouragement and the book (hope you like the books!); to Monkeygirl for being herself; and for everyone who shook hands with me and said, "An author? Cool! Don't give up, and congratulations!" or words to that effect. Thanks are also due to those who said, "Go. *Go*. How many times in life do you get the chance to do this?" and to the Prince and Little Princess for being supremely unconcerned. (They had bubbles to play with. *grin*) Thanks to Locus and the Science Fiction Museum for hosting the event. It was pure wonder, for me at least.

Last but certainly not least, thank you to my marvelous Readers, the reason why we all do this. Telling stories is hard work, but the perks are grand—and I'm so glad you're here to listen. Dawn has come up while I've written this, and I think I should make myself a cup of coffee, sit down, and have a few quiet moments before the little people awaken. I think I'm going to spend the time thinking about the strangeness of life, and how words can reach through time and space to change people's lives. Then I'm going to go back to writing.

My God. I love this job.

Top Ten Things I Wish Someone Had Told Me About Writing

July 6, 2006

Thursday. I promised a list of ten things.

Last night I went to a tango class with Monk. We had fun—at least, I had a tremendous amount of fun. Learning the tango is on the List of Things I Must Do Before I Die. Along with reading Henry Miller in Paris and climbing at least one mountain, the list is long and perilous. But a lot of fun. The thing I've learned about tango is, it's a social dance (as the instructor keeps saying). In ballroom you're socked in hip to hip and leaning away from your partner up top, so there's a tension *away*. In ballet, when you partner with someone you have to give them enough room to move, and you have to hit your mark, and it's just a different beast. But in tango you have to *lean* into your partner. The leader has to push the follower around a little, and the follower has to resist enough that she can tell where the leader wants her to go.

It's a fantastic lesson in listening with the whole body, and since I'm normally so bossy it's going to take me a little time to learn how to do it well, and it's also a tremendous relief. I danced with the teacher, with an older woman (I think her name was Rosemary, and she was wonderful) and with an older gentleman with a tractor on his shirt who tried to teach me how to bolero. And, of course, with Monk, who did very well for his fourth lesson.

The thing that turns this into a regular Thursday Revue is Elizabeth Bear's review of Holly Black's *Tithe*, which is one of the best YA fantasy books I've read in the last five years—and not only because Black did her homework, but girl can *write*. Dayum. Anyway, the review is spectacular, as most of Bear's work usually is. *grin* Add to more rumbling fallout from Plamegate, and you've got yourself a passel of reviews. Which leaves time for me to do what I've been threatening, and list the ten things I wish I'd been told about writing.

1. Writing is hard work. Don't expect it to be an easy way into a celebrity lifestyle. It's hard frocking physical and emotional work. Don't whine about how hard it is. Just do it.

2. People will assume you are your characters. That's fine. Just don't let *yourself* assume you are your characters. As Herbert once wrote: *on that path lies danger.*

3. Edit other people's work as gently, thoroughly, politely, and ruthlessly as you want your own edited. Treat your editors kindly—they want your work to sell, too.

4. Some writers think good work on your part means fewer readers for them. Hence, they will act oddly toward you—kind when you're struggling, nasty when you're successful. It's not you. The people who are just as happy with your success as their own are your true friends. Try to be like them, and be happier about your friends' successes than your own.

5. If you don't look at your old work and say, "Oh, God. I can do better than *that*. What was I thinking?", then you're not growing as a writer. Get down to it.

6. It's normal to want to strangle your characters. It's also normal to have no idea how the story's going to end. Just hang in there. Ninety-nine times out of a hundred it turns out fine. If it doesn't, put it in your slush pile. You can always come back to it later.

7. Write what you love, not what you think you *should* write. Life is too short to write something you hate.

8. It's okay to be a pulp hack. Some of the greatest writers ever (Shakespeare, Dickens, Hugo, Poe) were pulp hacks. Pulp hacks get paid, and they have fun, and they write truly for their readers. What's not to love?

9. Writing a novel doesn't teach you how to write novels. It only teaches you how to write the novel you're writing now. Writing a short story is the same, or a poem. Just focus on learning how to write the piece you're writing now. And the biggest, baddest rule of them all:

10. Do not give up. Do not ever doubt you have a story to tell. Never, ever, ever give up. Keep writing.

Of all these, Number 10 is the most important. As I tell my students: "If I could just hammer into your heads not to doubt yourselves, that each and every one of you has a story to tell and the ability to tell it," I would consider myself a successful teacher. Just keep doing it, over and over again, and do what you love.

Tell the story you love. The rest will take care of itself. I promise.

The Hard Sell Doesn't Work

September 8, 2006

I thought for a while about even mentioning this. No, really, I did—second thoughts are rare and wonderful things for me, but I do occasionally have them. The benefit of this kind of advice to new authors is infinite, though one suspects those who need it won't dig it until it's too late.

The advice I have to give is this: *Relax.* Because the hard sell doesn't work.

I've noticed this at conventions and signings galore. The new author, excited and happy, is pitching his/her book to everyone in sight. S/he assumes that because s/he is excited, all the rest of us *cannot* wait to hear about his/her novel/screenplay/short story/idea/self.

A little bit of this enthusiasm is good, it makes one's eyes sparkle and one's cheeks flush. You can't help but be excited about your own work—if you're not, you should find another career.

But beware the hard sell.

The hard sell is filling the airwaves with your self-promotion. It's consistently talking over other people to get your idea heard. It's bringing the discussion around to you and your work every time you open your big mouth. It's being so "cool" you literally don't care about anyone who doesn't register on your celebrity radar.

It's annoying. And it will lose you so many friends and opportunities it's not even funny. Publishing is really a small business. You never know when the person you're rude to on a convention panel or in an elevator at a trade show may hold the power of life or death over your wee manuscript in the future. It's best to be tactful and interested in other people at cons and shows, not to mention writer's group meetings. You don't have to be self-effacing—you can network until the cows come home and talk shop until you're blue in the face. But *don't use the hard sell.*

I'm going to give two instances of the hard sell, suitably embellished and altered to protect the innocent and the guilty alike. Ready?

Instance Number One: There's a certain small press—let's call it Hip Press—gathering critical praise for taking risks with horror and fantasy manuscripts. They publish some interesting stuff and their covers are good...but before an author submits to them, he asks around and finds out they suffer from a serious case of "I'm cooler than you." The managing editor (or the person impersonating him at conventions and trade shows) has rapidly acquired a reputation for snubbing authors who don't fit his definition of "hip" or "groundbreaking" enough. Which would be fine...except Too-Hip Editor is openly rude when he snubs. He ends up sneering both publicly and online at several paranormal authors, who quietly tell their friends in the biz (including their agents) that they won't submit to Hip Press, since working with this man will almost certainly turn into a nightmare.

The press struggles with low submissions quality and finally folds, and nobody will say out loud *why*. The answer is simple—Too-Hip Editor cut his baby off at the knees by doing the hard sell—"my press is so cool we won't publish *you*." He was so interested in his own "coolness" he shot himself in the foot professionally.

Instance Number Two: Imagine, if you will, a new author (let's call her Z) at a convention. She's just beginning to break out and is attending a number of panels. Z is so excited about her book she brings mountains of promo material, and everything that escapes her mouth in the panels is about how wonderful she and her books are. It doesn't matter what the subject of the panel is—Z is quite frankly all about Z and Z's books, and devil take the hindmost.

After a particular panel Z approaches a midlist author and makes her pitch for a collaboration. The midlist author listens politely and says something vague, then disappears. Z waits after the con for the people she exchanged business cards with to call or email, and sends emails to the midlist author reminding her of Z's presence.

There is no response, and Z's frustration grows. In response, she tries pushing her books even harder, but suddenly conventions are full and she can barely score a panel or a signing to save her life. Unbeknownst to herself, Z's behavior has been passed around by several midlist authors, and she's acquired the reputation of a blowhard. Nobody wants to hang with her, and she grows more and more frustrated.

Writing is not generally thought of as a social art. One of the biggest complaints one will hear from writers is that they must spend almost as much time marketing as writing. Done correctly, marketing and networking can be a boon and help grow your career. To be an author means one has to get along with editors, publishers, agents, fans, booksellers, and God knows who else, including convention staff. That's a *lot* of people to get along with, not to mention other authors, who may struggle with the same issues and be dying to talk shop with someone who understands.

Yet so many starting authors commit two great sins: they only flog one manuscript and they don't know how to get along in a professionally-social capability. The former belongs in another blog post, but the latter is what this post is all about.

Getting along professionally-socially is an art more than a science, and it's made more difficult by the fact that publishing is such a bloody incestuous business. You will meet everyone once or twice in your career at *least*. Your gaffes will follow you like crows follow the gibbet. Your offenses will be spoken of with relish and your coups may be envied.

The hard sell is the number one mistake I see new writers making in that capacity. Here's a few tips and pointers to help you along, if you suspect you may have inadvertently tippled into hard sell territory.

1. Write nice thank-you notes. In your thank-you notes, talk more about the other person than you do about yourself.

2. When you are on a convention panel, mention your work's title at the beginning when you are introduced. Then let it go. Don't mention the title again unless it's truly relevant to the panel and the discussion at hand.

3. Study arbitration and counseling techniques. Don't say, "You're an idiot" to someone. Say, instead, "I disagree because ___" or "It's my perception that ___." Not only will this avoid the hard sell, but it will make you look good, especially on a panel.

4. Be polite to everyone. It's hard, especially when you've had a six-hour plane flight and baggage problems and now you're at dinner with someone who keeps yammering about their newest success. Make the effort to be polite and to care. You never know.

5. Try to be just as interested in other people as you are in yourself. Yes, this is hard for every single human being. But just try it. Be as happy for others' success as you are for your own. There really is enough success to go round. Suzie Sue's success will not steal readers from you.

Your own idiocy will steal readers from you, not Suzie Sue's new book.

6. If you meet a famous author or one of your personal heroes, thank them kindly for their good work and fine example. Tell them in one sentence or less how much their work means to you. Do not mention your books/screenplays/novels until they ask—which they will, especially if you say, "Your work helped me continue writing. Thank you so much." They have people trying to pitch crap to them all day long. Don't do it. Your time will come.

7. When you are on a convention panel, limit yourself to one or two promo items. A cover illustration and a stack of bookmarks works just fine. A cluttered pile of promo material makes you look desperate.

8. If you don't have a valid question while you're in a panel audience, keep your trap shut. The panelists are there because someone wants to hear their opinions. Do not use your opportunity to ask a question to do a cheap shill for your unpublished manuscript. It's rude, and people do remember these things.

9. Do not get drunk with fellow authors unless/until you have a personal as well as a professional relationship with them. I would say, don't get drunk with fellow authors AT ALL, but I've broken that rule once or twice, with the Selkie. *grin*

10. If you find yourself saying, "I know you don't publish _____, BUT—", for the love of God, stop. Take a deep breath. Back away from the pitch and go soak your head. That one sentence causes new writers untold amounts of grief. If you find yourself using it, you should rethink your strategy a bit.

11. Be polite. Be polite. **BE POLITE.** Say please and thank you. Wait your turn. You may occasionally be run over by someone who is using the hard sell. It's frustrating, but it's okay. The person still using the hard sell will make

your patience, forbearance, and politeness look *ever* so much better. Do not be discouraged if you don't get a chance to talk to a celebrity. Console yourself with the thought that when you do finally manage to speak to a celeb or a famous author, your politeness will be a welcome relief for them, and may lead to good things.

12. Be careful where you gossip. Yes, scuttlebutt travels fast in the publishing industry. But don't go around gossiping indiscriminately. You'll hear more if you keep your mouth shut, and when you do decide to drop a quiet word of warning to a fellow industry person, it will carry more weight.

13. Last but certainly not least, use a little common sense. A pinch of sense goes a long way in this biz. You will find more friends and make more connections that endure with politeness than you ever will with the hard sell.

Apocalypto, or, How Many Snuff Films Will Gibson Make?

January 2, 2007

Usually, dear Reader, I like to accentuate the positive. This may come as a surprise to readers of the Valentine series (or even of this blog). But really, when it comes to other people's creative efforts I usually like to remain silent unless I really enjoyed the creative effort in question. There are enough people writing shoddy Amazon reviews out there; unless I can wholeheartedly endorse spending time and effort on a book or movie I generally like to keep my mouth shut.

I am about to break that rule with a vengeance. Consider yourself warned.

Yesterday, it being the New Year and me being in need of a little entertainment, I did something I should not have done. I went and saw Mel Gibson's newest cinematic offering, the one that's been showing up in previews for at least a year now.

I thought—now, please, try not to laugh—that there might be some redeeming qualities to it. Seriously, I thought at least it would be visually interesting, and I'm always up for some good visual Muse food. After all, *The Cell* was a terrible movie (Jennifer Lopez should be ashamed of herself for ruining such stunning visual collages with her lack of acting talent, but then anyone who will date Ben Affleck is probably suffering from a severe and quite possibly congenital lack of judgment) but it had Vince Vaughn and Vincent D'Onofrio, and some of the most beautiful and eye-wateringly great visual effects I've seen in years. All in all, a movie best played mute, with dialogue added by one's possibly-stoned or certainly-drunk friends. But I digress. I gave *Apocalypto* the benefit of the doubt. I should not have.

The movie opens with a wild-tapir hunt that ends in gore. We're introduced to Maya hunters who would feel right at home in any tailgate party, playing practical jokes on each other and doing some good old fashioned Mom-and-apple-pie red-meat eatin'. Just a bunch of dudes hanging out in the jungle, yo. They go home after bringin' in the tapir meat (I ask you, was the testicle-eating sequence REALLY that necessary, Mel?) and party it up with the li'l women, complete with bitching mother-in-law and barefoot, pregnant, and doe-eyed wife. Ah, life in the sticks. All these guys needed were banjos.

Enter Bad Guys, a bunch of dudes from the squalid, festering city who are about to enforce their city-mouse morals on these innocent country-mouse children of Eden. The dudes from the Big City are Very Bad People, and in case we had any ambiguity on that score AT ALL, the director treats us to fifteen minutes of gore, gore, murder, gore, rape, gore, brutalization, gore, tugging-on-heartstrings, gore, gore, and did I mention the gore? Pregnant wife and aw-shucks little kid are left in a "safe hiding place"—i.e., a hole in the ground—and Our Plucky Hero, Jaguar Paw, is dragged off in captivity for a few of the worst days of his life.

The plot cobbles together bits of the *Rambo* and *Mad Max* films, although those films were done with a modicum of humanity, or at least an enjoyable lowbrow energy. Gibson now wants us to re-envision these silly plots as the grand stuff of glorious epics. Set in among the

Mayan civilization, the movie opens on some scrotum jokes, and then continues with a penis joke. Our good tribe of hunters are a happy people, content to hunt and make babies and make fun of each other's willies. But an evil tribe comes along and kidnaps all able-bodied folk, ties them up and drags them to a slave market. We know they're evil because they cackle a lot and sneer at the misfortune of others (if they had moustaches, believe me, there would be twisting).

Plucky Hero and long-suffering friends are subjected to various ordeals by Bad Guys who are cartoonish villains in Mesoamerican drag, complete with leers made more fantastical by tattoos and earplugs. Plucky Hero, it appears, has a Destiny, which is hammered into the long-suffering viewer's ears and eyes by a number of ham-fisted attempts at Foreshadowing And Subtlety. We are treated to more nightmarish gore on the way to the Big Putrid City, where, it quickly becomes clear, the heapin' helpin' of gruesomeness already dished up was an appetizer to the wide and varied banquet of disembowelment, stabbing, shooting, exsanguination, and ho-hum dismemberment (not to mention beheading and corpse-desecration) our humble director had in store for us.

Let's move along with the plot, shall we? Plucky Hero is Saved From Grisly Human Sacrifice By a Fortuitous Solar Eclipse, and if the sarcasm is dripping through my capitalizations here, please be assured it's warranted. After another utterly pointless sequence of gore (the captives, instead of being saved for a ball game or for further human sacrifice at a later date—because apparently the Mayans didn't believe in conserving potential sacrifices they went to All That Trouble to obtain—are dragged off to be sadistically killed in pairs) the *deus ex machina* sets Plucky Hero free to run home to his wife and kid conveniently left in that hole in the ground (remember them?).

There's just one problem—the Very Bad Guys don't want to let this one go, despite the OODLES of captives they're apparently bringing in (and if we didn't believe the oodles of captives, the mass-grave scene would have laid ALL our doubts to rest with yet more over-the-top sickening gore).

Then it's Plucky Hero versus the Very Bad Guys, with God (or at least a sadistic scriptwriter) on the Hero's side. We're treated to clubbings, drownings, knifings, massive trauma by spiked tapir-trap, death by conking yourself on an underwater rock when you're foolish enough to dive off a waterfall—and lest you gals feel left out, there's an underwater birth scene complete with the peril of being a) drowned like a rat in a water barrel or b) clobbered by the Very Bad Men who are chasing your Plucky Hero Husband.

The fun just never ends.

The most galling thing about this waste of celluloid (or electrons, since it was shot in digital) is that it might have been faintly affecting had not the director's obsession with messily killing people (not to mention his ham-handed Catholic preaching) interfered. After all, the jungle is beautiful and the lavish production budget gives us color-saturated vistas and extras numbering in the thousands, all painted, bedecked, tattooed, and ear-plugged, not to mention nose-plugged, to within an inch of their lives.

Gibson leaves no cliché unturned in his effort to drive home that Jaguar Paw is the hero, that the guys chasing him are mustachioed villains, and that his Poor Preggers Wife (named Seven, because all the other nifty names were taken and what woman in Mel Gibson's universe needs an independent personality OR a decent name?) is a paragon of Marian virtue and long-suffering obedience.

The movie should have been visually stunning despite its director. It should have had some emotional impact. Instead, it's reduced to the faintly queasy feeling one gets after eating too much corn dog and seeing a bad sprint race—or a rodeo, which at least has the virtue of having no stunt doubles. Poor Rudy Youngblood (Jaguar Paw) actually has some acting ability and a mighty fine pair of buttocks displayed to great effect in the wet loincloth he spends the entire movie in. (That's another thing—Mel, honey, what IS your fascination with the naked male bottom? The ratio of boy booty to bazoombas in this movie is SADLY off.) Dalia Hernandez (Seven) is just aching to bust out of the two-dimensional June-Cleaver-in-the-jungle straitjacket Gibson's put her in. (The birth scene alone qualifies her for Megatough Bitch Points. If she'd been dragged to the city, you can bet your tootsies she would have had no truck with this *escape* BS. She'd have taken the damn place OVER.) Jonathan Brewer (Blunted) tries to give us a great performance, but is cut off (ha ha) by the script's unmerciful cascade of dick-jokes aimed at his character. The shaman-dude (I can't remember his name, being bludgeoned into uncaring by the point it appears in the movie) is much more interesting than anyone in the film, being the only one with a halfway-real motivation. The Big Bad Guy, the foil to our Plucky Hero, just looks bored through his leer despite glimmers of what could be talent just yearning to breathe free.

It's a shame to see both nascent ability and natural beauty maimed by such a lame lack-of-script overweighted with heavy, panting moralizing and even heavier blood and guts. I'm fully aware that I write books about a katana-toting bounty hunter with an itchy trigger finger and a violent life. I've battered my Watcher heroes (not to mention Delgado in *The Society*) all to hell. I even watched *Kill Bill* for inspiration while writing *Working for the Devil*, you know. Really, violence in movies is kind of my cuppa tea.

But the violence in *Apocalypto* isn't even pointless. It's *beyond* pointless. Not to mention the fact that the ending is utterly, totally, completely, and in all ways lacking any shred of believability. As The Gods Are Bored and an archaeologist both point out, in one of the film's few peaceful moments the Spaniards (read: Catholic missionaries) are shown coming ashore A GOOD THREE HUNDRED YEARS BEFORE THEY EVER SET FOOT ON SOUTH AMERICAN SAND.

Ardren[3] says it best: *But I find the visual appeal of the film one of the most disturbing aspects of "Apocalypto." The jungles of Veracruz and Costa Rica have never looked better, the masked priests on the temple jump right off a Classic Maya vase, and the people are gorgeous. The fact that this film was made in Mexico and filmed in the Yucatec Maya language coupled with its visual appeal makes it all the more dangerous. It looks authentic; viewers will be captivated by the crazy, exotic mess of the city and the howler monkeys in the jungle.*

And who really cares that the Maya were not living in cities when the Spanish arrived? Yes, Gibson includes the arrival of clearly Christian missionaries (these guys are too clean to be conquistadors) in the last five minutes of the story (in the real world the Spanish arrived 300 years after the last Maya city was abandoned). It is one of the few calm moments in an otherwise aggressively paced film.

The message? The end is near and the savior has come. Gibson's efforts at authenticity of location and language might, for some viewers, mask his blatantly colonial message that the Maya needed saving because they were rotten at the core. Using the decline of Classic urbanism as his backdrop, Gibson communicates that there was absolutely nothing redeemable about Maya culture, especially elite culture which is depicted as a disgusting feast of blood and excess.(Is "Apocalyto" Pornography, Traci Ardren)

Remember my rant about readers not being stupid? This movie exemplifies, with each headcrack, knifing, and over-the-top cliché, WHY I wrote that rant. Granted, the average cinema-goer goes to the movies to be entertained

---

[3] http://archive.archaeology.org/online/reviews/apocalypto.html/

and in some cases anaesthetized. I plead guilty on that count—sometimes I just want to see some explosions and car chases. But when even a lush tropical setting and genuine acting talent can't save a bundle of clichés from crashing and burning under the weight of a director's sadism...well, I'm not entertained. I'm just faintly nauseated.

It was so bad that at the very end, when the palm leaves shut and the jungle swallowed Plucky Hero and No Longer Preggers But Still Barefoot Obedient And Doe-Eyed Wifey, I half expected blood to burst out all over the leaves after a few seconds of transparent-ploy peace. The credits came as a welcome surprise and relief, being the best part of the whole bloody movie. I left the movie theater with a sense of nausea that cannot be explained by the tub of popcorn I munched during the gore-and-brain-spattered spectacle. I was so utterly unmoved by all the cartoonish violence that I had no trouble eating my popcorn.

I *was* nauseated by the idiocy of the script, the utterly brainless colonialist moralizing, the ham-fisted attempts at foreshadowing, the ease with which millions of dollars was wasted on something which could have been valid in another director's hands but which just turned out to be another reason to lampoon Mel Gibson's self-important sadomasochism on *South Park*. I'm a big fan of bad movies. I love B-movie shlock with a passion. I go to the *Rocky Horror Picture Show* and I devour the *Evil Dead* movies and I love utterly wonderful, horrible films like *Reefer Madness* and *Attack of the Killer Tomatoes* or even *The Brain That Would Not Die*.

But *Apocalypto* isn't a movie. It's an engorged jungle snuff film. It's two-plus hours of exploitation made even worse by the fact that it could have really meant something...if Mel Gibson had kept his goddamn mitts off it, or if he'd been on speaking terms with reality.

When we started seeing previews for this, the Selkie snorted, "Just an excuse to film *The Patriot* on another continent." If that was all, it would have been mildly enjoyable despite itself. Instead, insult is added to injury and topped with bloodspatter.

Will someone please revoke Gibson's directing license and make him go hunt and gather on his own little plot of fundamentalist heaven? Preferably with someone to spank him for being a bad, bad boy, because that's what all his "movies" seem to be asking for. *Apocalypto* is utterly without redeeming value in a way I thought only pornography could be. To think I actually paid for my ticket. Ugh.

Other reviewers might find something of value in that steaming mess. After all, it's subtitled in ancient Maya! That's got to be worth something, right? Nope. Even the subtitles and the lush greenery couldn't save this one. It's a shame, too, because I'd love to see this kind of resources thrown behind groundbreaking films spotlighting the complexities of indigenous peoples worldwide. What I got was a too-stupid-to-be-believed pile of violent moralizing bullcrap.

End of rant.

The only advice I can offer is: cut this pile of poo a wide berth, because the stink doesn't end when you leave the theater. Ugh.

Letter to a Young Writer

July 17, 2007

N*ote: this is an actual email I sent in reply to a cry for help last week. I think it's useful, so I'm posting it with identifiers stripped out.*

From: Lili Saintcrow < *************>
Date: Jul 14, 2007 9:50 PM
Subject: Re: Lili, I Need Your Advice!!
To: **********

Hey ******,

This is going to be fast, since you're under deadline and I pulled an all-nighter last night.

There are two problems here. One, you're afraid. That's okay. Inside every writer's head is a little voice that says, "You're not good enough. You can't say that. Who the fuck do you think you are?" For me it's my mother's voice. "That artsy fartsy shit will never put food on the table! Grow up!"

EVERY writer has that voice in their head. It is the Censor, the curse of every creative, and it's also a crutch when you don't want to work or when you're pushing your comfort boundaries.

What helps me is knowing I can write absolute crap. Giving myself permission to write crap was the best step I ever made as a writer. You can write whatever the hell you want. Quality isn't important. Quantity is. You churn out enough work and sooner or later your craft will get better and someone will like something you've written. It's the shotgun theory of publishing. So just-okay writers get published because being just-okay at this is all right. Even being crappy at this is okay. What is important is that you try.

*******, I hereby give you permission to write the worst dreck in the multiverse, as long as you write SOMETHING. When you finish reading this, get your ass in the chair, put your fingers on the keyboard, and just go. Don't worry about whether the writing is any good. Right now that's the least important fucking thing on the planet. The MOST important thing is sitting down and getting the shit out, so that you can see where you are and correct your aim if you're not where you want to be.

Writing is like sex. Even bad sex is mostly better than none. You just have to a: show up, b: be flexible, and c: have a good time and enjoy yourself. You enjoy yourself and give pleasure through writing, and the rest will come.

Second of all, you have your own idea of how the story is going to go. Can it. You're not telling the story. The character is. Throw out everything you've plotted out about this character. Outlining is only useful so far. Get out of the fucking way and let her tell the story, and give her permission to go off the beaten track. Your idea of what will happen will most likely end up being the furthest thing from what actually happens. If I may be permitted to stretch the "writing as sex" metaphor (which I wouldn't do if I wasn't certain you'd understand and we're good enough friends that you won't take it wrong) I'd tell you: you can't have an orgasm when you're all tense. It's a delightful accident you need to calm down enough to let happen. The same thing happens with the character.

To sum up:

1. Let the Censor yammer all s/he wants. Just sit down and write.

2. Even by writing absolute crap (which I highly doubt it will be) you are still doing more than most "writers" dream of by just sitting the fuck down and getting your finger on the keyboard.

3. You can write crap. It's okay. The first million words you write don't fucking matter. Let them be however they want. You wouldn't expect to do a marathon or firing a gun perfectly without practice, right? Writing is no different. It's okay to suck for the first million words or so. (Note: you generally get better in that first million words. Don't sweat it.)

4. Throw out the outline and let the character tell the story, not you.

5. Have some fucking fun with it and relax. Just like sex.

There. That's all I have time for right now, I'm about to crash. But this is IMPORTANT. If you have to, write out:

THE FIRST MILLION WORDS DON'T MATTER.

Tack it up over your computer. Just do what Stephen Brust says. He has this written on a sign where he can see it while he's writing:

AND NOW, I'M GOING TO TELL YOU SOMETHING *REALLY* COOL.

Works for me. Really, it doesn't matter if it sucks. What matters is getting the words out, again and again.

Now get your ass off email and go write. Set a kitchen timer for twenty minutes and just write. Don't worry about whether or not it's "good" who the fuck cares? It's your story. Just get it out.

Then do it again. With breaks for the bathroom etc. as necessary. *grin* Or a colostomy bag, if you want to.

Didn't I tell you to get off email and go write? *wink*

Good luck,

     Lili

On Lucifer, Research, and Faith

January 4, 2008

I got another piece of amusing hate mail today. Now really, I expected some trouble with the subject matter I write on, and titling the first book *Working for the Devil* was hardly guaranteed to be a peaceful choice. But could people at least do their research before frothing at me?

My portrait of Lucifer borrows from a few traditions, not the least of which is the Gnostic and Grail traditions that show Lucifer as a green-eyed, possibly liberating angel, with an emerald set in his forehead. That emerald is intimately connected with the Grail tradition (is it annoyingly hilarious that I'm only enjoying reading *Holy Blood, Holy Grail* these past few days? I think I was too young the first time I blazed through it). It also borrows heavily from S. Jason Black and Christopher Hyatt's work and to a lesser extent, from legends of the Nephilim—the original rebels, you might say. And Cathar theology, the idea that the world is flesh trapping a spark of spirit, held a significant place in early drafts, but didn't survive the challenges to such duality inherent on a polytheistic worldview.

The thing that irritates me is people writing me to tell me I'm "wrong" about the Devil. *sigh* I did a lot of research and reimagining. If you don't like my version of Lucifer, fine. I'm okay with that. But don't presume to tell me I'm "wrong" based on current fact-and-research-free evangelical Protestant cant. I'm drawing on a rich array of sources to reimagine what demons might be in a non-Christian setting, what demons originally were conceived of as, etc.

It might surprise people whose only research into the idea of Lucifer is televangelist horsepuckey to know that the "adversary" was originally a Judaic theme, the angel who functions as the Left Hand of God to test the faith of mortals. The term "demon" comes from the Greek "daemon", a guiding spirit that accompanies a man through his days. (Philip Pullman, notably, references this in the *His Dark Materials* trilogy.)

Still, I suppose it shouldn't surprise me. I was ready for this sort of reaction the instant I realized what sort of themes I was dealing with. It just irritates me when people tell me I'm "wrong" without bothering to do any research themselves. I suppose it's a knee-jerk reaction springing from what they're culturally comfortable with and unwilling to look beyond. I *understand*, and understanding breeds compassion—I just hate being told I'm "wrong" when the person mouthing off clearly hasn't read any of the source material.

The core assumption I take issue with is that I haven't researched Christianity. Which is *obviously* not true. I began a period of intensively researching all major world religions when I was about twelve, and I still follow that interest today, two decades later. I did my best to read the source materials and the holy books, as a part of my own spiritual process of figuring out what exactly *I* believed. (Note: still an ongoing process.)

As a result, I found out pretty early that much of what I'd been raised to view as "Christianity" was really an accretion of political and economic compromises masquerading as dogma, springing from the Catholic Church's (long-term and briefly, historically speaking, successful) attempt to grab temporal and financial as well as spiritual power. Reading the Gnostic Gospels, Arianism and the Nicene Creed, the Cathar "heresy" and the history of Byzantium and the Fourth Crusade (just to name a few subjects) opened my eyes to a number of issues still reverberating in Christianity today.

One might guess, correctly, that I have little use for the blind faith in the sects of Christianity—Catholic, Orthodox, OR Protestant—enjoying a lot of popular support today. Nor do I have much use for the current popular form of Islam, mostly because of its attitude (mostly as an echo of social forces, since the Koran takes a different view) toward women's rights and scholarship/science.

Other "world religions" have their drawbacks as well. Most organized religions seem to exist for one reason: to financially fleece their faithful and provide a thought-free refuge from the scary unpredictability of the world. Providing pre-digested pap to one's followers in order to blind their capacity for critical thought and empty their pockets has never struck me as a mark of "spirituality" or even of a developed ethical framework.

One can, in my treatment of fanaticism and the Republic of Gilead, discern a lot of my attitudes toward the current theocratic trend in America today. One can even discern my feelings toward "gnosis" or personal experience of the divine rather than church-mediated contact with the numinous. But don't presume to tell me I haven't done my research. I thought long and hard about each aspect of the "Devil" I utilized. I may be guilty of drawing the wrong conclusions, but it's not for lack of thought OR research.

Once one gets into issues like this, who can judge what the "wrong" conclusions are? Taking a page from the Montague Summers playbook won't help your case if you honestly expect me to take you seriously.

You needn't worry about my soul. It's just fine where it is. I welcome responses to the books as art, and I welcome thoughts on the reimaging I did and my utilization of these long deep strands in Western thought and history. But don't serve up some Revelations-laden tripe you got off TCN and expect me to be impressed or even to respond. You don't like my version of Lucifer? Fine. Write your own, or read someone else's version. There's a lot of them out there. Almost as many as there are versions of God out there. Feel free to pick your own. I actively encourage such behavior. Just, you know, do some research first. Please.

Over and out.

Writers, Well, WRITE

April 14, 2008

There's still reverb going on about my Friday post at Fangs, Fur & Fey[4]. Some people are still not reading 90% of the post—they're just skimming until they get to one particular thing and then hanging all sorts of things on it. *sigh* Ah, teh interwebs.

Go ahead and get out the pitchforks. Because I *don't* believe just anyone who has an idea for a book they're going to write someday when they have time is a "writer". There are people who like to call themselves writers for one reason or another, and I was posting about what separates them from the people I call writers—the ones who do the goddamn work. If you don't agree, fine. The world is wide enough for both of us to call parts of it what we will. Who cares about the opinion of a barely-midlist hack anyway?

It is an unpopular thing, to state that one must have hard work and discipline to be a writer. A lot of people are overlooking the fact I said over and over again in the comment thread (because it was off the point of the post) that *once* you have built up your discipline you can "take a day off" and your busy little brain will continue to work on the story. Daily discipline will carry you and it DOES carry several professional writers, including a few who brought

---

[4] http://fangs-fur-fey.livejournal.com/357510.html

that up in the comments. But discipline absolutely needs to be reinforced and cared for just like muscle tone. Move it or lose it. It is fragile, and it is easy for it to succumb to timesuck. In all the hubbub, I did not see anyone advocating another specific route that would do what I said writing every day does, to wit:

- You give yourself the clearest possible signal that this work is not going to go away, and you are committed to it.
- You bolster the habit of just sitting down and putting your hands to the effing keyboard.
- You give yourself the opportunity to practice hard enough and long enough to start producing readable product.
- You give your writing a priority to match other priorities in your life.

Some people took issue and umbrage...but they didn't bother to offer an alternative that would satisfy those things. If you have a Sooper-Sekrit System that will give you those benefits without writing every day, good for you. Go do it. Don't wait around to tell me how wrong I am, just go do it. You've got the jump on me, sweetheart. Use it. There is no magic flexible bullet that will grant you writing success. If I told you there was, I'd be lying.

But you know, it's a lot easier to be successful the more professional and prepared you are, and discipline is part of preparedness and professionalism. I would be irresponsible and untruthful if I didn't say it. You can hit the ball out of the park on a fluke, yes. But it's a lot, lot easier if you've trained for it and showed up at the bloody park when the game's on.

A lot of people like to pretend "writing" is some sort of super-classified Arte you have to Suffer and have the Magic Ingredients for, which are jealously guarded secrets only available to NYT Bestsellers. It does serve a lot of ego to act like this stuff is FM (Fucking Magic, for those of you not married to a mechanical engineer.) Saying, plainly and clearly, what I believe about professionally writing strikes to the heart of that dynamic—I'm attempting to *deobfuscate*, with my Friday posts.

Writing, like any creative endeavor, ain't simple and it ain't easy, and there is no magic key—but hard work and persistence can prepare you for whatever magic there is to happen. I don't have a lot of use for most of the stuff Natalie Goldberg said (there was a lot of complicating the simple in there) but one thing she said did particularly stood out, for me. It was about sitting at her typewriter and looking out the window, and feeling a rush of Joy and Love For All Things. When she told her teacher this, thinking she had hit some sort of enlightenment, he simply said, "Quit stalling. Get back to work." (I'm paraphrasing, she wrote it better.)

And on that note, dear Readers, I'm going back to work.

Tell Them All to Sod Off

May 16, 2008

re there any new writers in the audience? Young writers, or those who are just starting out? Come a little closer and sit down in front, you guys. This one's for you.

Welcome to writing. It's a hard job. I think it's one of the best jobs in the world. But it is so easy to be blown off-course. There are a lot of reasons why you'll tell yourself you can't write. There's the *I Don't Have Time* reason. There's the *I'm Not Good Enough Yet* reason. There's the *Everyone Will Laugh At Me And I'll Only Be Rejected Anyway* reason. There's the *Words Never Come Out Like I Want Them To* reason. And millions, billions more.

There is one thing I want to tell you about, something absolutely critical to a writer. It's the ability to give the whole bloody world the finger. You know which one I'm talking about.

That finger.

Look, this is not an easy job. But it can be done. You just won't get anywhere if you let any of those naysaying voices, whether they're in your head or coming from someone else's mouth, stop you.

Lean in, guys. I want to tell you something important. **It is a thousand times better to write something crappy than not to write at all.** I am deadly serious. The worst bit of talentless dreck full of "that"s and passive verbs is better than shooting yourself in the foot before the race is even started. It doesn't matter WHAT you write. It matters only THAT you write.

I've had a couple teachers tell me they have their students read my writing posts. (I'm honored, by the way.) Hello, kids. It's good to have you along. Here's the one thing I want to tell you: **Don't you ever, EVER let anyone stop you from writing.**

Go ahead and feel afraid—it's okay to be scared. (The power to transform the world is incredibly frightening, isn't it?) Let fear drive you to say the things that need to be said. Let it be fuel. Keep writing. Just keep your fingers on the keyboard, keep the pencil on the paper. It will all turn out fine, I promise. I swear. Just keep writing.

A work doesn't have to be perfect. If a perfect novel was ever written the universe would probably implode from the antimatter or something. We are imperfect beings in an imperfect world. Just get the writing done. Get the work out on the table, and then you can cut it up and edit it and prettify it.

First, as a very wise writer once told me, *you write the goddamn novel*. Then you worry about everything else. A lot of new writers think they have to edit and polish as the damn thing is coming out of their heads. As you get better at writing a lot of editing will go on in-process. But often, new writers will fall into the trap of second-guessing every word, and they get frustrated. Nothing comes out right. The words just won't do what they want. And they quit.

You don't have to get that frustrated. Focus on getting the work *out* first. There's plenty of time for revisions. Believe me, you'll revise the damn thing so much you'll be sick of it. Have fun and don't sweat while you're actually writing it, at least.

Then there's that other reason to quit: other people. Or other people's voices in your head, saying *You can't do that!*

You can't SAY that! This is horrible! Who do you think you are, anyway? Everyone's going to laugh at you!

I call that little voice the Internal Censor. It's hard not to be so self-critical that it seems safer to just let the blank page lie there. It's hard to push those voices aside. It's achingly hard to believe you have a story that needs to be told when the world seems designed to tell you you're insignificant. Young writers have the hardest time of all, sometimes, because they haven't developed that sense of proportion yet—the one that tells them, however faintly, the self-critical voices are full of horsepuckey.

Hey, don't get me wrong. The sense of proportion doesn't get louder when you get older. Sometimes you just learn to listen to it, that's all. If you can, if it will help, give those nasty voices the old finger. Tell them to eff off.

You have a right to write.

You further have the right to write whatever the hell you please. So it's not Shakespeare or Chekhov or the famous Great American Novel. So what? Every word you put down, every day you're at the keyboard or holding the pencil, is better than a day of being too afraid to do it. Don't ever let anyone tell you that you don't have the right to write. If you love writing, if it burns in your soul like a rocket, even if you just enjoy it and feel compelled to do it, *you have a right to write.*

Don't stop because that naysaying little voice in your head tells you it's not good enough. Don't stop because Aunt Martha would be *so* embarrassed if she knew you were writing THIS! Don't, at bottom, write for anyone else.

Hey. Psst. Lean in just a little closer, because I'm going to whisper. This is Sooper-Sekrit. Write to please yourself. Write what you want to read. Write what makes you feel good. Write what makes you tingly. Write in any genre you damn well please. Write cross-genre. Write about whatever you want to.

Yes, yes, you do have to worry about grammar and structure and story and characterization and making your work readable. That's why this is an art, that's why this is work. But at the heart of this work is joy. If you write what you love, what pleases you, your work will have a ring to it. It's like fine crystal. It sings. Even if it's sloppy. Craft can be learned. With enough patience and persistence you can learn when to dangle your participles and cleft your gerunds. You can learn the rules, and they will help you. But the joy, it's a gift. Don't throw it back in the Universe's face by writing what you think you *should*, or what someone will Approve Of.

Write whatever makes you happy. Put pen to the paper, put pedal to the metal, lay down some tire-rubber and streak for the horizon. Race to beat the Devil. Do it because it feels good and it's what you want to do.

Those voices always come back. I don't think I've ever met a single writer who didn't have them in his or her head. Get practiced at telling them to sod off. Learn to distinguish those voices from honest critique or emotional blackmail. Critique you can accept gracefully, blackmail and drama-queening you can walk away from. But the self-critical voices? You can just give them the finger. Yes, *that* finger. Tell them to fuck off. If nothing else, it's tremendously satisfying. In this line of work, we take our satisfaction where we find it.

All right? You dig? Now. Go write what you love. Don't let anyone stop you. Laugh in the face of fear, even if your heart is cold and your knees are knocking. Go set fire to the words you were given to write, the words only you can say. Go out there and give 'em hell.

Embarrassment Is Relative, or, Writing Those Smexxors

May 23, 2008

I think you're going to enjoy this post, dear Reader. It's about smut.

Due to the volume of mail I receive, I often can't respond to fan letters—or I'd spend the day doing nothing else. But often, fans ask Questions, and I do my best to answer those questions in a blog post.

A Reader sent a particularly intriguing question a little while ago, and I beg indulgence for only now being able to get around to it. The question was, *don't you get embarrassed when writing sex scenes? As a fellow writer, I often do. How do you overcome embarrassment?* As I started writing my response, I got into a whole-enchilada post about sex scenes in general. Ahem. Enjoy.

I guess I'm lucky, since I have a writerly friend—the Selkie, aka Mel Sterling—who's very comfortable writing erotica (and in some cases, outright PWP, but only if a good friend asks her to). We've discussed all sorts of issues, from word choice to the ideas of consent and restraint, and what makes a sex scene work. During one particularly memorable discussion we were at a restaurant that had linen napkins, and as she is an inveterate fiddler, my friend had rolled her napkin up very tightly and was using it to accentuate several points. Not to be left out, I'd done the same. But, erm, when you roll a napkin up like that, how do you stop it from flopping? You fold down the end a little, so it looks like—yeah. We were playing Dueling Phalli with linen napkins. Much to the amusement of everyone in the lounge, I might add. But we were so into our conversation we barely noticed.

Writing a sex scene, or a chunk of smut, is kind of like that. If you pause to think, "What in Christ's name am I DOING? Aunt Martha would SO NOT APPROVE!", you're going to lose a lot of, ahem, steam. Smut-writing is a lot like sex—most of it is showing up and paying attention, lots of it is making yourself comfortable. Here's a few things that help me when I have to, er, Get Some Nookie In That Book!

- **Find some Hawt Music.** Like one of my personal favorites, the White Stripes' "Ball and a Biscuit". Lots of Rolling Stones. I like grungy guitar and bluesy stuff to Get In The Mood, but it might be different for you. Get music that makes you think of desire. No, not sex—desire. Trust me on this. Sex scenes aren't really about the *consummation*. They're about the *desire*. Even in erotica, the purpose is to titillate the reader; that's pure desire, not consummation. (Note: Pure erotica is a different beast than a sex scene in a novel. There. Disclaimers done.)

- As the Selkie says, attend to the smutte every bit as carefully as you'd attend to any other aspect of a story. **Just because it's smutte doesn't mean it's not worth writing well**. I really can't add more to that.

- **Get yourself comfortable**. You don't have to dress up to write a sex scene. If you're wearing something that pinches and binds, it might have unpleasant consequences for the fiction. It's possible to write a totally hawt smexxor scene in sweats and a T-shirt, with kids screaming in the next room. I've done it. Also, you can light a scented candle or some incense, put on some nice music that relaxes you, take a bath beforehand and think about it. Get yourself in the mood just like for a combat scene. The two are remarkable similar. *Comfort* is the key concept here. You have to be comfortable enough to concentrate and to write. Do what it takes to get there, to maximize your comfort level. (But don't let comfort-seeking become a timesuck. All things in moderation!)

- **Let it be part of the plot.** If two reasonable adults would be having sex in that situation, go ahead and let them. Don't try to shoehorn smut in where it doesn't belong, but don't engage in gymnastics to keep the characters apart OR together. Unless, of course, the plot calls for it. Or unless you're writing a comedy.

- **Get rid of the idea that everyone will think you like what you write.** Or more precisely, try writing about stuff you don't necessarily like in bed. There are a few authors whose sex scenes are THE SAME in EVERY BOOK, so you can kind of tell what they might like in the sack. I don't know about you, but that's something I'm happy not knowing about a great deal of humanity. Give your characters interesting quirks. Have them try things you wouldn't try. It's cheap, fun, and safe experimentation. It will give you a little bit of necessary distance that might help ease some embarrassment. Here's a big secret: most readers couldn't care less. Really. Just give 'em good writing and a good plot. Don't get yourself all twisted up in a knot thinking they might Know Something Shameful about you. *They don't care.* They just want good fiction.

- **Do some research!** Read a few romance novels, try to find a sex scene you like. Read some Anais Nin. Sample some Anne Rice. (If you can stomach it.) Watch some hot, steamy movies. (No, I'm not thinking *Basic Instinct*. I'm thinking *Original Sin*. I'm thinking *Kama Sutra*. I'm thinking *Frankie and Johnny. Scent of a Woman. Bleu.*) Get a copy of *The Guide To Getting It On. Now*, analyze. What about these things makes them "steamy"? What qualities do they share? If they don't work for you, why? If they DO work for you, why?

- **Don't go for the cheap shot**. The Selkie and I are in agreement about this. She pointed out this morning that good smut *should* NOT be pornographic, and by that I mean it should not degrade or abuse. There are legitimate cases where a writer may want to portray abuse or degradation, but in those cases they should not be meant to cause an erotic reaction in the reader. I read a few scenes in Simmons's *Carrion Comfort* that skeezed me *right* out. They were meant to, and they involved sex, but they weren't sex scenes. Sex in a book is like in real life: it has a variety of uses and purposes. Be very clear about the type of scene you're writing and what the purpose of sex in that scene is. It'll help.

- **Use the words that are right for the scene.** Words are your tool and your craft. Think about the words you're using for sex scenes and the precise meaning you want to convey. The Selkie notes: *I used to say I'd never use the C word because it had been so abusively used in my experience, but I've just written* *the pr0n where that IS the right word, because of its connotations for the character and the story's intended audience.* Never say never when it comes to any word.

- **Don't be gratuitous**. As the Selkie says, *sometimes a fade-to-black IS what is called for.* A lot of my sex scenes are actually very lightly described, because I aim to let the reader decide how detailed s/he wants it. One of the few fights I got into with an editor was over the gratuitous insertion of a sex scene. I balked. The editor said the Readers would feel cheated if I didn't slap a sex scene in. I still refused—one of the number of times I can count on one hand I outright refused to do something an editor suggested. I am not ever going to put a sex scene where it doesn't belong. I'm just NOT.

- **It ain't personal, honey.** Well, everything you write is going to be personal, because your word choices are like a fingerprint. But you can't consider your sex scenes as being *too* personal. Get over the idea that Fannie Mae and Brucie Goose (i.e., the general public) are going to be giggling behind their hands at your sex scenes. They've got Jerry Springer, the tabloids, and their own sex lives to worry about before they can worry about yours. Just get on with your work.

- **Write your embarrassment**. Okay. So you can't write the hot smexxors without dying of blushing Victorian-style heaves. There's a way around that—give one of your characters hideous embarrassment. Make him impotent, make her afflicted with the giggles, make both of them fumbling around hitting their head and deciding to move to a bed. Look, sex IS embarrassing in real life. It's damp and weird and makes funny noises.

You need practice to do it right. If you are having trouble doing a totally-hot smexxor scene, have it turn out a little less than perfect. Get sand in someone's bikini. Have someone fall off the bed. You and your characters will both learn something. (Heh.) Then, after you've finished and written a few more scenes, you can go back and tweak the embarrassing bits piece by piece, making them less embarrassing for the character. Voila! Instant hot-hot love scene. (I have used this SO MANY TIMES. There was one incident with Dante and Japh that—oh, never mind.)

- **Use all your senses**. Sex is a total-body experience. A lot of the best sex scenes I've ever read weren't even particularly graphic; they just described sensations—what things felt, tasted, smelled, looked, sounded like. This is where the power and habit of *observation* I'm always talking about comes into play. When you find a sex scene you like in a book or a movie, pay attention to the sensory details. What makes it so good for you? What makes your heart race and your palms sweat?

- **Do It Anyway**. Look, I'm still mortified when I have to write a sex scene. I just buckle down and do it anyway. The book is important enough for me to do so. Just hold your nose (ha ha) and plow through. There's always room for revision.

- **For God's sake, think about what you're doing**. Sex in a book is like death, combat, red herrings, or dialogue. It has to have a *point*. Don't just ram a sex scene in because "books like this have to have a sex scene." Genre conventions are there to be played with, subverted, stood on their head, juked-out, and "had fun" with. Go ahead and play with expectations. Give us a sex scene that's not like every other sex scene. Give us something to think about.

- Last but not least...I have often said **the best writing comes from what you're afraid of**. So your heart is in your mouth and you're terrified? Good. Use that. You're hearing the little voice saying "so-and-so would be so DISAPPOINTED in you for writing this"? That "this is true but you shouldn't say it"? Good. That's ROCKET fuel. Some of the best writing comes when we're staring at that sort of fear and using it as a spur. Go ahead and break boundaries. Write what makes you afraid and uncomfortable. Look that demon right in the face and call it by its name. Later, when you're sweat-soaked and shaking, and your reader looks through it and says, "Damn, that's some good writing. Where'd that come from?" you can say, "Aw, shucks, tweren't nothin'." Don't stop writing a smexxor scene, or any other scene, because you're afraid. Fear is a sign there is a rich vein of experience and emotion to be mined. Get your pick and shovel and get to it.

To Spec vs. Organic Novels

May 30, 2008

Let's talk about structure. Or more specifically, dear Reader, let's talk about writing a novel to specifications ("to spec", like a category romance or a specifically-genre book) and writing what I call an "organic" novel[5]. One is not inherently better than the other. They're *different*, and serve different purposes. I write both, and I think any writer has to know those different processes. Let's talk about writing to spec first.

Writing to spec means you're given a specific project. For example, right now I'm working on a category romance (lovingly titled *Weasel Boy*) with a pretty tight length and subject requirement. In order to effectively write this book, I have to both:

- Know the things the editor/publisher/readers are going to expect
- Make myself comfortable within those strictures/structures

I also have to perform the hat trick of writing to spec, which is *knowing* which rules I can break. Which is just another way of saying I have to find something new within those strictures/structures, something all my own.

---

[5] I'm writing about novels because that's the form I'm most comfortable with. You can substitute "short story" or "poem", etc., if you like.

Writing to spec requires a fierce discipline. I've always said romance writers, and category romance writers in particular, are some of the most disciplined writers on the planet. They *have* to be. They have an incredibly tight structure which includes length requirements, genre convention, aiming within their subgenre, nookie level (as in, how much nookie the reader/publisher expects), and particular expectations about the ending (an HEA, *Happily Ever After*). You can find comparable discipline in the Western genre and also in the category-suspense (think Mack Bolan) genre as well, though the romance genre has the blessing of being bigger business with a fair number of interesting backwaters/subgenres.

The length requirement alone will give some writers kittens. Say you have a length requirement of 70-75K. You don't have a lot of room for subplot, long-winded description, dead weight. Every word needs to tell, and you're going to get better at making every word pull its own (and its neighboring sentence's) weight.

Working within those constraints teaches a writer *a lot*. Then there's convention. You need to know the conventions of the genre you're working in when you write to spec, and know them thoroughly. You need to know how much convention-breaking you can get away with, which requires a sense of your audience's needs and expectations when they pick up the book.

This requires not just reading within the genre, but reading *critically* within the genre—looking under the hood of the popular books, seeing why they work and where they don't, what you would do differently, what unspoken assumptions and expectations are part of that genre or subgenre's mythic "set". It's learning a language, if you will, so you can break its grammatical rules effectively.

I write the *Watcher* books largely to spec, because they are intended to be identifiably paranormal romances. They have a specific pattern and a specific language, and they require a different set of mental "muscles" than, say, a Kismet book or the Valentine series.

Growing a novel organically is different. A major difference rests in the idea of genre. Writing to spec means you're aiming at a genre, which is really just a collection of story markers to help readers find your book in a bookstore. Gestating an organic novel means you often don't find the genre it belongs in until after the damn thing is born (and sometimes not even then).

For me, writing to spec is like following a blueprint. Producing an organic novel is like excavating an archaeological site. I have very little control over what the characters decide to do, and the structure of the novel follows its own dictates. If writing to spec is an act of sensitivity toward one's audience, then writing organically is an act of submission to the creative process. I may have an idea of where I'm going to end up, just like I know I'm eventually going to die, but the intervening journey is largely a surprise.

I can knock out a to-spec book topping at 80-85K in a month and a half, taking into consideration the time needed to do a couple drafts and pass it by a beta. I don't need more than a week's (or so) worth of "cooldown" between them. On the other hand, an organic novel has a definite gestation period before I sit down to write it, and it takes four to five months to produce a workable rough draft, of whatever length the story demands. Then there's the snapback—a considerable period of recovery, because I don't just write an organic novel, I *experience* it on an emotional level. It takes a heavier emotional toll.

I think the emotional toll/involvement is the reason "organic" novels tend to be cross-genre or hard to fix within the constellation of genres. Feelings are messy, and organic novels tend to be complex, both on a thematic and an emotional level. (At least for me.) That "messiness" tends to situate the "organic" book in weird crossdrifts between genres.

I think the key to working to spec is wordcount and structure. You've got to think about what you're doing, and why, and why it works in the confines of the story. You have to know what each scene is intended to accomplish, which genre/subgenre "markers" you need to hit, and you need to get a consistent wordcount out each day to keep momentum.

Conversely, the key to working an organic novel is wordcount and "fuel"—you have *got* to keep your emotional/artistic well full in order to cover the withdrawals you're going to be pouring into the story. An organic novel tends to require a lot more "artistic" fuel—those things that feed your Muse so she can work. (For me, it's schlocky action movies, or knitting, or low-light photography, or reading a book I'm not picking apart for structure.) Those things that make you feel renewed, no matter what they are.

Wordcount is important for spec work because you have to produce a disciplined product. It's important for an organic novel because the dry "hump" in the middle-to-last quarter of the book can literally kill the work if you don't keep chewing at it in little bits. It can be distressing, to say the least, to reach that point in an organic novel where you just have to trust the work not to fail you, and if your well is dry you might end up just throwing your hands up in despair. That doesn't get the book *done*.

The joy in writing a to-spec novel is performing within a set of rigid constraints, like interpreting and performing a piece of classical music—there's a set of rigid expectations you have to find freedom within. The joy of writing an organic novel is following the creative process for the hell of it, like a freeform jazz jam session—the rules are still there, but you're playing faster and looser with them. It's all good music, and both are satisfying to pull off well, but they require different types of effort.

There's a tradeoff between the two. Writing to spec will strengthen your discipline and force you to really, really think about plot, structure, reader expectation, and lots of nuts-and-bolts things that will make your implementation of organic novels that much technically better. Writing organic novels will teach you all sorts of weird stuff about characterization and your own creative process that will inform your spec work with the stamp of originality it will need to become more than just a potboiler. It's totally possible to botch either a spec novel or an organic novel, and fixing botches in either will help you fix botches in the other, for a variety of reasons.

I think both processes are necessary for a writer, though each writer may have a personal preference about the type of novel they prefer to write. Myself, I tend to alternate— I don't feel right if I'm not producing at least some spec work, and spec work gets awful, awful tedious if I'm not producing an organic novel at the same time. Of course, this is my opinion. Feel free to take with grain of salt.

Just When You Hit 40K...

Taken, known privately to me as *Weasel Boy* (which is, I've not yet said, a category romance containing were-wolverines), hit 40K recently, and I'm thinking of how I'm going to wrap it up. I am struggling with the urge to go back and excise bits that might not be working quite right. I can pretty much tell it's a timesuck work-avoidance mechanism. The book is resistant, like they always are (for me) in the middle. The only way through is just to put one's head down and get the damn words out.

It's a lovely gray rainy day here, and I've finished a couple of books. The first was *Mao, The Unknown Story*. This is a biography of Mao, but not your usual "the man was a Red saint" bio. For one thing, the picture presented of Mao Tse-Tung is that of a smart, functioning sociopath whose quest for power sacrificed literally everyone in his way and a great deal of his fellow countrymen as well.

I could have done with a little more analysis of how such a military noob got control of armies, but I am well aware it would have made an already-long book into a doorstop. Mao seems to have risen to the level of his monumental self-love, double-dealing, and thirst for power. I have little difficulty believing the man was, for lack of a better term, an asshat.

I also have little difficulty believing the controversy over the somewhat un-academic nature of the book's structure and sources. But truth (or so-called objectivity) isn't solely found in academia, and when you're dealing with a repressive regime that will still kill to keep its founding myths endorsed, of course you're not going to name your sources so the bloody hatchet men can find them.

I would have like a bit more about how exactly Mao kept power in the Party, but I'm not familiar enough with the Communist apparatus exported in the 30s-50s or with Chinese social norms and strategies during that timeframe either to pick up on what the authors could have given me contextually about that issue. That area of study will have to wait until I finish with Charles II, the French Revolution, and Disaster Capitalism. (So much to find out about the world, so little time...)

Pretty much the only difference between Mao and Stalin is that no Kruschev has yet arisen who finds it expedient to lift the curtain on Mao's transgressions against humanity. Mao seems to have been slightly better than Stalin at using the resources of the state to starve and terrify the population—or maybe his statistical "pool" was bigger so he could kill more with the same strategies. It's a toss-up.

In any case, the book was a good read and I was interested all the way through. Though it was seriously depressing, and it's led me down many a mental primrose path contemplating the connection between the majority of people who thrive in politics and the psychological profile of the criminal sociopath.

The next book, kind of a palate-cleanser, was Tom Robbins's *Fierce Invalids Home From Hot Climates*. True to form, Robbins has served up another looping foray into philosophy, thinly disguised as a novel. While the pedophilic subtheme was enough to squick me a little (Robbins is no Nabokov, but sometimes even Nabokov was no Nabokov, if you know what I mean) the book was still incredibly enjoyable, and I devoured it in two days when I should have been writing more and reading less. I particularly enjoy Robbins's idea that a sense of humor (and a refusal to take oneself seriously) is a hallmark of evolutionary advancement, and any book that marries the idea of neutral angels, the CIA, the Third Prophecy of Fatima, and a South American witch doctor with a pyramid-shaped head is bound to be a good time. Especially in Robbins's hands—he fiddles Dame Grammar like a man who loves Her, and gleefully violates story rules with a sort of puppy-like abandon that's hard to shake a disciplining finger at.

Other readers might get exasperated with his run-ons and digressions, but I'm more forgiving of that sort of thing when the author has my attention and is performing interesting hat-tricks. Oddly enough, I cannot read Palahniuk (except *Fight Club*) but I really have a great time with Robbins, and their looping sentence structures really strike me as very similar. Go figure.

If my review of *Fierce Invalids* seems a little light on plot, that's because trying to boil down the plot of a Tom Robbins book without trying to rewrite and explain the whole damn thing is useless. I'll content myself with saying the book follows its hero, Switters, around through a series of events that are logical in their own way and yet extraordinarily fantastic (in all senses of the word).

The *only* problem I have with Robbins is that women are a mystery to him. But I think I've only read one or two male writers who can really write a female character, and it's no shame to admit a boy is mystified by the Female. (It is, after all, our prerogative to mystify.) Plenty of male writers end up using the female as an Other, a receptacle for all sorts of weird sexual dreams thinly covered with social commentary or philosophical hogwash, and completely overlook the fact that women have an interior life/exterior existence of their own, divorced from the male gaze. I suppose you can do that when your gender is considered normative and the other half of humanity's considered the aberration on all sorts of levels, primal and otherwise.

Still, there's a big difference between a male writer who genuinely likes women and is okay with being mystified (Robbins) and a male writer for whom women are a dangerous mystery that must be controlled or beaten down so the male psyche can survive (like, for example, Bukowski, especially in his more misogynistic moments). The quality of work may be superlative (I really enjoy reading both Robbins and Bukowski) but the differing treatment of female characters is sometimes enough to make a girl wish for some literary dynamite and a grammar bazooka, not just a room of one's own.

Okay, I'm dragging Woolf into it, so it must be time for me to end the ramble. I'm kind of eyeing my TBR pile and wondering what to dive into next, and I pretty much have it narrowed down to the bio of Charles II OR another attempt at Jeffrey Eugenides's *Middlesex*, which both the Selkie and Make_Me say is superlative. Choices, choices.

Random, Quick, and Dirty Ways to Write Better

June 6, 2008

Five Random Bits of Writing Advice

1. **Get the Prom Queen to the dance before cutting her up.** Or, as I like to call it, *get everything out so you have a whole corpse to perform surgery on.* This means nothing more than just writing the damn piece, no matter how bad you think it's going to end up being, before you start cutting and chopping on it. A lot of new writers (and even some old hands) get in the middle of a book/piece of writing and then decide to go back and change the beginning. Over. And. Over. Again. This is pure timesuck fueled by fear, and most of the time it isn't necessary. Getting the whole book out, no matter how crappy you think it is, means you have a view of the whole story arc and can *then* go back and prettify the beginning with an eye to punching up the end.

This is different than realizing a book just isn't going to go anywhere, that it's dead on the vine, or deciding to work on something else for a while. One should hopefully learn to differentiate between all those seductive little speedbumps. But try not to go back and endlessly revise unfinished pieces; or if you do, be very conscious of what you're trying to accomplish and whether or not it's timesuck.

2. **Kill fucking passive voice.** Passive voice is weak and wishy-washy. *She was sitting* or *Cathy was running*? No. She RAN. Cathy SAT. Passive verbs often creep in when the writer is unsure, either of the material or of the total wordcount. Unless you can make a good case for absolutely needing the passive voice, kill it. Step on its head before it breeds and get an active verb in there. You want your stories to breathe and move and flex. Burying them under an avalanche of passivity is not going to help.

3. **Send in the man with the gun.** Can't figure out what happens next? Kill someone. Rough someone up. Throw in vampires or zombies. Make it worse for your characters. Often you *do* know what happens next, and are avoiding it for some reason. A good zombie attack (or other disaster) will shake some things loose, and if all else fails, it's fun, when a piece isn't behaving properly, to add some screaming and combat. You can always take the screaming out later, if you really want to.

Don't worry about pacing so much in the first drafts. It is easy-peasy to *slow* a book down. Descriptive phrases, a bit of reflection on the hero/ine's part, a little bit of passivity. Getting a book to move faster is the hard part, and if you have a choice, opt for action. You want your reader wondering what the hell is going to happen next, not yawning and thinking "this is a good place to put this hunk of paper down so I can go call Grandma."

Also, a lot of new writers are afraid to be too mean to your characters. Don't fall into that trap. If there is not a real risk to the characters, how is the Reader going to connect with them, feel their anguish, fear for them? *If* there's no real danger, there is no real emotional reward for a hero/ine, and no place for the Reader to connect. Rough 'em up. Beat 'em down. Make those damn characters WORK.

4. **Readers, dear Writer, are smarter than you are.** If you find yourself saying—or even thinking—"But you don't *understaaaaaand!*" to your critique partner, reader/reviewer, editor, etc., take a deep breath and go soak your head. When you come back, realize *it is YOUR job to communicate clearly.* If nine out of ten readers don't get your Deathless Genius, you have not done your job. Tthere are always going to be folks who don't "get" what you're trying to convey, and there are always going to be naysayers and doom-monkeys who won't like any piece of fiction they didn't personally stamp with their Purple Velvet Seal's Ass of Approval. That's just the way it is, and your work is not going to be for everyone. There is no "one size fits all" within genre or without.

But if more than three people tell you a scene or a motivation ain't workin', honey, you need to reconsider. Even if it's your most-favorite-est scene in the whole damn piece, even if it makes you sigh and cry every time you read it, even if it's survived numerous revisions. You may just have to murder that darling. Put it in a dump file and you can possibly resurrect it later, or just reread it in the dead of night when you need a little pick-me-up because the world's not in love with your heartbreaking, staggering genius.

If I sound sarcastic and sharp here, believe me, it's for Your Own Good. (And mine, too.) Writing is hard enough without letting an overblown ego make it harder. If those hoi polloi you're expecting to fork over cash for your prose don't understaaaaaand, then you need to find the way to communicate more clearly. No matter how much you think you already have.

5. **Believe, believe, believe.** Never doubt you do have a story to tell. There are stories lined up around the block for you and only you—stories that have chosen you to tell them. Some of them are promiscuous little buggers (fairy tales, hero tales, tragedies, myths) who still want your

stamp of originality, the nuance and attention only you can give. Others are weird little children who have your eyes, your nose, and your quirky half-smile, and they're waiting *just* for you to put your fingers to the keyboard and give them breath and life. The stories are always there, crowding in around you, peering over your shoulder. Part of the discipline of everyday writing is so they know you'll be there, same bat-time, same bat-channel, so they can form an orderly queue and wait their turn.

Don't worry if a million other people have done the same thing. If you quit worrying about being derivative you have more energy to devote to making the story your own—giving it the emphasis only YOU can give. Who cares if fifty million people have written and rewritten *Beauty and the Beast*? I'm going to have fun writing MY version, thankyouverymuch, and I invite and enjoin you to write your own. If nothing else, it's good practice for structuring a story. You have a right to write, and you have a story to tell. Sometimes the head gets so crowded with naysaying thoughts that it might not seem like there's much of value in there. But do not ever buy into the notion you don't have a story to tell. There are stories lurking behind every saltshaker, every blade of grass, every raindrop. Relax. They'll come out and play—if they can trust you to sit down and spend time listening to them.

As a bonus, I think I'll throw in an extra word of advice. Whenever you find the word "that" in a manuscript, STAB IT AND KILL IT. 9.9 times out of ten, "that" is unnecessary and just weighs a sentence down. Argue with each and every "that" you find. There will still be plenty of them left over—I'm of a firm belief "that"s are like cockroaches. They *breed*. Just like wire hangers and solitary socks.

Hack Manifesto

June 13, 2008

Good morning. I hope you're comfortable? Good, good. Have a cuppa, settle in.

This last week I was informed that my writing advice was utter crap and nobody wanted to hear it because I am a hack. As my friend Neutronjockey from LiveJournal pointed out: *I believe the word "hack" is derived from the horseworld. A hack being a reliable, trustworthy, hardworking—I believe it was specifically referring to a horse used for work rather than pleasure. While I won't deny you pleasure-use...there is certainly nothing wrong with being a hack.*

Damn skippy. There is nothing wrong with being a hack. To that end, dear Reader, here is my Hack Manifesto.

My advice on writing is geared pretty specifically toward people who want to make a living at it. It's also geared to people who love language and want to tell a ripping good story. It is not for Artistes or for fragile speshul flowers who want only squeeful strokes for their delicate, heart-shattering, mindstopping genius. Go read Annie Dillard or Natalie Goldberg if you want to hear how haaaaard writing is on the Delicate Flower.

Here in my writing world, we work, and we work hard. We get our hands dirty. We take our goddamn rejection like adults, we buckle our belts tighter, and we get on with producing the best manuscript possible on several fronts.

That's what being a hack is—taking pride in your craft, taking pride in producing something people can use and love.

This is the heart of hackdom—creating things people can enjoy. You *can* write utter crap and get away with it. But that's not what the true hack does. Writing fiction that is supposed to show how smart you are or how you're treading the path of High Litrachur is a fool's game—literature disappearing up its own asshole, so to speak.

The hack's purpose is twofold: 1. To produce the best writing possible; clear, vigorous, and working prose easy for the reader to understand. And capable of carrying hundreds of pounds of theme, symbolism, plot, characterization, and all the workings of a good story effortlessly—WITHOUT BORING THE READER BY HOW FUCKING SMART YOU *THINK* YOU ARE. This is very important. The best writing is not hard to understand. It is *deceptively* simple. We are in this business of writing to communicate. That's what writing is, *communication*. Your communication is dead on the vine if you're not looking to be clear and reasonably concise.

There is a fair degree of art in being reasonably concise and as clear as possible. Clarity is not just using the appropriate word—it is using the appropriate sentence length, giving enough detail to build the scene but not enough detail to choke the unwary reader in a morass, pacing appropriately, and pruning away all that lovely writing you've perpetrated without a clear idea of what it's for.

There's another aspect to this: consistently producing what a reader will enjoy reading. I'm not saying you have to stick to hackneyed trends because that's what Everyone Else Who Has Succeeded In The Genre has done. I'm saying you need to understand why a genre is the way it is, why myths and fairytales work, the rules of the form you're working in. You have to know HOW the engine works before you can go tinkering with it to make it work better. You can't just slap crap on the page and expect people to worship you.

If your business is to tell stories, you need to know *how* stories work so you can pick the appropriate parts to jam in their engines to make them run without sticking and backfiring.

2. The second purpose of the hack is **to have fun**.

Yes. Fun. Look, if you're not enjoying writing, or not enjoying WHAT you write, what the hell are you going to do it for? This is not a line of work where it's possible to dink around and make a living. Precious few writers, even hacks, do this for the money. IF you want to make a living doing this, you MUST enjoy some part of it or you're going to end up with a serious ulcer and bitter, bitter nastiness in your soul.

Plus, there is that indefinable quality of joy in some work. If I'm not having fun on the page, how the hell can I expect the Reader to? I don't just mean the shallow fun of explosions and titties, nice as those are. I mean the soul-deep joy of creating something that's as good as I can make it. I mean a *ripping* good yarn, a story the Reader gets emotionally involved in. I don't care if the Reader laughs OR cries OR gets angry OR suffers with the characters OR gets angry at the characters. I'll take ANY of those, or ANY other strong emotional reaction. If the Reader has that emotional reaction, that kick from the story, *I* have done my job and created something useful. That, my dears, is my idea of FUN.

The hack understands people are not going to consistently fork over their hard-earned cash to read mental wanking that doesn't work for them. The hack wants to create something people will use. If it's a romance novel that makes a Reader sigh, if it's a Western that makes a young girl smell gunsmoke, if it's a doorstop of fantasy that makes a fanboi happy inside, if it's a novelization that draws a Reader back into the world of a movie or a telly series they loved so much—all of these are noble, worthy pursuits. These are things worth doing *well* for the Reader's sake. Without the Reader, a writer is just shouting into the wind—and while a certain degree of shouting into the wind is good exercise, there comes a point (sooner than you think) when shouting is just sound and fury signifying nothing but an overblown ego.

Part of being a hack is being professional. A hack comes in on or under deadline, understands an editor really just wants to make a story better, knows critical reviews (even the ones that are just sour grapes from a jackass who chooses to review instead of writing his[6] own crud) are valuable in their own way, and is constantly looking to make their work better.

A hack understands the fine balance between obeying the conventions of a genre and slipping a hand under genre's skirt to tweak ever so gently at those conventions— all to provide an enjoyable experience. (*snickers gently*) A hack *can* engage in stunt-writing, as long as s/he has a clear idea of why/how to break the rules. But a hack will not expect others to bow down to their Deathless Genius.

A hack *takes pride in the work*. A hack does not take pride in the size and firm plumpness of his or her ego. Here's another statement some people are going to take issue with: I firmly believe each and every artist who deserves the name is a hack. An artist has a hack's work ethic and a hack's understanding of the form they're working in.

Those without the work ethic, those who do not expend the effort, are artistes, dabblers, dilettantes. There is nothing wrong with artistes, dabblers, and dilettantes. They're just fine, they're okay, and there is nothing pejorative in those terms as far as I'm concerned. I simply

---

[6] Or her. Gender bias, thy name is English.

save my admiration for the hacks because I understand how hard they work.

I am proud to be called a hack—the same way I'm proud to be called a bitch. A bitch works hard and takes no crap from anyone, is assertive, and has self-esteem. So does a hack. (Which, tongue-in-cheek, beggars the question of whether I'm a bitch hack. *snerk*) Dickens was a hack. So was Dumas. So was Shakespeare—his funky butt got PAID for the work he produced, and he understood WHY the plays worked. (He still gave off some stinkers, but given the political climate he was working in, no wonder.) Zane Grey is just as valid as Jane Smiley, and I think they're both hacks because they both figured out something that worked and kept/keep refining, reinventing, and making it work still further. Louis L'Amour? Edgar Rice Burroughs? Alice Hoffman? Edgar Allen Poe? Barbara Kingsolver? Anthony Trollope? Jack Kerouac (even in his more nutty stimulant-laced moments)? Stephen King? Others too numerous to list? Hacks. Proud hacks. Hacks I'm proud to read. The quirk that considers some of them "fine litrachur" and others "damn hackdom" is merely an accident of media taste. Or the taste of some hoity-toity reviewers.

Yes, I'm a hack. A hack is dependable, responsible, faithful, hardworking. A hack is in love with language and determined to produce the best story they can. A hack is enjoying herself to the hilt while churning out good prose. So, goddamn hell yeah, I'm a hack.

I would not want it any other way.

Defense of Genre and Artistic Compression

June 20, 2008

I woke up this morning with a serious case of the crankies. If I seem a little bloody-minded, dears, that's why. I had a whole post about genre planned, but it would probably devolve into a huge slaughter of innocent verbage, full of recondite brimstone and unfounded combative assertions. Such is my mood. I'll content myself with two small things this Friday and go vent some of my spleen in fiction.

First, I'd like to make a small observation. An overwhelming number of what we consider "classics" today were seen as "genre" or "trash" fiction in their time. Novels were considered women's reading (and hence, unSerious) for a very long time; plenty of novelists were supposed to feel ashamed of their success. Lots and lots of things we see as classic (because they have survived) started out as, for want of a better word, schlock.

This hinges on a theory I have that lit fic—the "highfalutin litrachur" genre is supposed to be the redheaded stepchild of—is actually a pretty recent invention. The Selkie and I were talking this over last night and she observed that lit fic is actually so diffuse it can't be pigeonholed into a genre. There's a fair amount of accuracy in that observation. I wonder if that diffuseness makes it easier for critics and reviewers to drown it in academese and impress each other, therefore making lit fic "serious" and genre "unserious".

The second thing I'm going to mention is artistic compression. I use this term to describe the sense of pressurization I feel right before I dive into a big project—in this case, the fourth Kismet book. The outside world becomes an irritation and chores are something to be rushed through so I can get to the real work, which is the boiling of the book inside my head until it's ready to slide out at varying speeds. Ugh. That's a nice mental image, isn't it.

The sense of compression often returns, as Caitlin Kittredge so aptly describes, near the end of a book. (She calls it "Hibernation Mode".) A lot of the creative process seems to involve varying feelings of pressure. There's the pre-boil of a book, the stages of writing (including the MY GOD THIS BOOK WILL NOT DIE slog halfway to three-quarters of the way through) and the sudden decompression after a book is finished, which involves a lot of spinning aimlessly.

There's a sense of pressure in revisions too, and sometimes after a particularly intense round of revisions I feel drained and bug-eyed as if I've just rewritten the goddamn novel.

It is really, really important to think about those feelings of pressure and to identify one's own creative process, so it isn't a huge deadly thing each time. A lot of writers seem surprised each and every time by the intensity of the feeling and the emotional drain. No doubt it is surprising, but not analyzing the feeling and reminding oneself that it's normal can lead to a whole lot of inefficient flailing. While I enjoy a good inefficient flail as much as the next person, there's always the timesuck factor involved.

Figuring out your emotional reaction to your artistic process is one of those things that can make you a better writer—or at least, a more productive one. If you're not blindsided by the compression, if you can take a deep breath and remind yourself that this happened the last few times you worked on a project, the physiological effects (mine include sweating hands, headaches, backaches, feelings of crankiness only rivaled by PMS, and a great deal of synesthetic irritation[7]), while not receding in intensity, can at least approach the realm of something you can deal with instead of a Huge Fricking Unworkable OMG Problem.

I tend to view the creative process as a technician. If I can figure out how this engine works for me I can get, if not standardized, then at least *consistent* results out of it, which is what I want. I know a True Artiste is supposed to wait in agony for the numinous descent of the fickle Muse, but I don't have time for that. I've got books to write NOW, dammit.

---

[7] I use this term loosely, of course. Most of the time my borderline-synesthesia is a happy fillip to daily life, a source of joy and creative connections. But there comes a time in the compression cycle when it just gets to be too much input and I get seriously frazzled, feeling like a delicate sensory instrument being mercilessly whacked by reams of static and messy data pouring in. GAH.

On YA, Bullshit, and Low Expectations

July 11, 2008

First of all, I'd like to wander from the usual Friday routine and announce that I've sold (or rather, my lovely agent sold) a three-book young adult series, titled *Strange Angels*, to Penguin/Razorbill. Book 1 is done and book 2 is in the works. I'm really happy and excited to be working with Razorbill, and I'm thrilled to be branching out into YA even though I was terrified, while writing book 1, that I was Doing It Wrong.

I have pretty strong opinions (now *there's* a surprise, right?) about YA books, but mostly as a reader. I know what I like and I know what I don't like in the genre, and it's stayed pretty much the same (with a few thematic fiddles and indiscretions) since I was about nine years old.

First, there must be either no BS or low BS. This is especially crucial in a YA, since kids have, by and large, exquisitely sensitive bullshit meters. They may not be able to put their finger on why, but kids know when an adult is being false. They may not be able to do anything about other adults who lie to or BS them, but they can certainly not buy or read a book. I think it's critical not to BS any of your readers, because they will catch you every time. But it's even more crucial not to talk down to, lecture, dissemble to, or try to "snow" young readers.

Besides, how can we expect kids to tell the truth when adults lie to them? I'm not talking about tact. Or about saying, "This is something I'm not discussing with you because it's an adult conversation." I'm talking about flat-out lying just to shut a kid up or take advantage of them. Kids get bombarded with that all the time, and they get just as sick of it as adults do. The difference is, adults can do something about it (most of the time) and kids are helpless.

Example: I remember feeling utterly victimized when a specific YA novel I read completely bombed on the question of teen sex. The Virginal Heroine was vindicated in the face of a nasty whisper campaign and the Bad Girl Who Had Sex was in a car crash and terribly disfigured. Even at the tender age of twelve I had some problems with equating sex to disfigurement, especially when the same boy had been pressuring both girls for nookie—and he ended up with the Virginal Heroine, too! I never read anything from that author ever again, and I still shudder when I think of it.

I think there's a huge difference between explaining to kids about *appropriateness* and lying to them, or brushing them off because of their age. My kids expect reasonable and honest answers to their reasonable and honest questions. Sure, it sucks sometimes to have to explain some things. But that's why parenting is a JOB, you know.

I think it's incumbent upon the YA writer to be on the lookout for, and avoid, usual adult cop-outs when dealing with kids. There are plenty of YA novels that insulted my intelligence even when I was nine years old—and I very much conflate BS with an insult to the intelligence of the reader.

Next, I like my YA to be fully characterized. I don't like one-note teen characters any more than I like one-note adult characters. People are multidimensional, and I expect

109

at least a little ambiguity, motivation, and quirkiness in my protagonist. Too many people in the genre seem to think writing for teens means short sentences, short words, and short characterization.

This ties in with another thing—vocabulary. I don't think a YA writer should bend over backward to get the "current slang" in. (I about hurled a recent YA across the room when I came across a character saying, "Fo shizzle!") There's a certain level of faddish slang that will irrevocably date a book; and unless you are certain your book's appeal will survive being so dated, you should think carefully about your slang. Plus, most kids I knew growing up didn't give a rat's patootie about the "in" slang. We just said "cool" or "dude" occasionally.

Speaking of vocab, please for the love of God don't think that teenagers can't understand long words. Erudition and large vocabulary are not merely adult traits. Part of the reason I started reading "adult" books—as in, lit fic and SF/F for an adult audience instead of YA—very young was because the "teen" books I had access to back in the benighted 80s had Afterschool-Special vocabularies. I wanted new words. I LIKED going to my dictionary and finding new words, and my other reading friends did as well. (I've never lost that habit.) Kids like reasonable expectations in their fiction—they like to *rise* to them, not sink to the level of a brainless puddle of pseudo-slang word vomit.

Of course, I could be writing the world's worst YA and not know it. (I fully admit this may be the case, and it's not just because I feel like EVERY book I write is hideous in the first-draft stages.) But I know what I like, and what I've liked for over two decades when it comes to the young adult genre. It's authors like Sarah Dessen. Robin McKinley and Patricia McKillip. Anne McCaffrey's Pern series, her *Restoree* and *To Ride Pegasus*. Andrea Siegel's *Like The Red Panda*. Ursula Le Guin's *Wizard of Earthsea*.

Katherine Paterson's *Jacob Have I Loved*, Russell Banks's *Rule of the Bone*, Cynthia Voight's *Dicey Tillerman* series. Peter Beagle's work. LJ Smith's *Forbidden Game*, *Dark Vision*, and *Night World* series. There's some damn fine writing, right there. Those are books that didn't lie to me when I was young, or made me remember what it was like to be a teen or young adult. That's the type of book I want to write.

It's anyone's guess whether or not I'll be able to pull it off. Finishing up this monstrous Friday post, I'd like to mention what Jeff Soesbe says about low expectations.

Jeff points out that as a new writer, or a previously-unpublished writer, you do have to prove you know the rules before you get the leeway to break them. I've met a few "writers" who think the rules shouldn't apply to their Deathless Genius. Who believe that the world is too stupid to give them their due—which includes adoration and no editing or feedback. And lo and behold, they do not get published. Go figure.

Story Rules, and When to Break Them

July 18, 2008

Story has rules just like painting and drawing have rules, just like music has rules. In all art, you must first know the rules[8] before you can break them effectively—if you even want to break them. Here are a few (just few) that have helped me.

The Story May Not Belong To The Hero. As Karen Fisher says, *the story belongs to the character who changes the most.* It's okay for the story not to really belong to your hero. You just need to understand who the story really belongs to so you can provide resolution. Or you could rewrite the whole damn thing, making "the character it really belongs to" your protagonist. Your choice. Of course, spending time thinking about who the story really belongs to in the beginning stages can save you a lot of grief. I'm just sayin'.

The Arc Of Doom. Stories follow a pattern/arc. First, there is a situation in equilibrium, at rest. Then something happens to smack the situation out of equilibrium. There is conflict while the situation tries to

---

[8] Sometimes they're not rules, they're more like **guidelines**. Still, disregard at your peril, my dear word-pirates.

resettle itself. There is a crisis, then the situation settles into a new equilibrium.

Think about the equilibrium at the start of the book and at the end. Think about what the crisis point is. This crisis/catharsis is mostly what gives a satisfying emotional experience to the Reader, which is what you want. In order to manage that impact, you need to think about where it's going to hit.

Risk, Danger, Cost. If there is no *real* risk to the characters, there is no *danger*; there is also no *cost* for overcoming the obstacles. Without risk, danger, and cost, the story is not going to have as effective a crisis. If there isn't a risk or a cost, the characters are just doing things to do things, and the story runs a much bigger chance of collapsing like an unfortunate quiche.

You *cannot* be afraid of hurting your characters. Come on. They're not your friends. They're your *characters*. Rough them up. Make them risk something. It's all fun and games until some character loses an eye. Then it's *serious* story.

Made To Be Broken, *Sometimes*. Sometimes you can play with the rules. But be absolutely sure you know what rules you're playing with and what the intended effect of breaking them is. A great deal of thought and care must be taken with breaking rules.

When done right, it's what art is all about. When it's done wrong, it breaks a story—sometimes irretrievably. There are few things as hair-tearingly frustrating as that. You don't have to be a slavish follower of convention. A certain amount of internalizing and analyzing the rules of the road will let you decide how to break them in the way that best serves the story—or, more commonly and usefully, how to use them to uncover the heart of the story.

Oddly, the above are rules I rarely break, but just having them inside my head while I structure a story is neverendingly helpful. The biggest part of breaking rules is in grammar, especially for dialogue. People rarely speak

113

grammatically, and the way a character breaks grammar rules while speaking is a cheap, easy, and effective way to characterize. You get a lot of bang for your buck in the violation of grammar conventions. But that's another blog post.

Be safe out there, my friends. *ebil grin* Except for with your characters.

The SECRET
(or, There Is No SECRET)

August 1, 2008

On the train to and from San Diego, of course there had to be socializing. (You couldn't get away from it.) Last night I picked up the Teen's friend, Squeaker, from his grandparents' house. Both my conversational partners on the train and Squeaker's grandparents wanted to know the same thing. And no, it wasn't about my facial piercings.

It's the question I get all the time. *What's it like to be a writer?* Of course, this question means a different thing each time it's asked. It's the original Proteus. Sometimes it means *where do you get your ideas*, sometimes it's *how many hours a day do you write, where do you find the time*, or it can even mean, *is there a SECRET to it?*

Most of the time, it does mean the last. People often think there's some gold-edged mystery that, once solved, will lead to fame, the NYT Bestseller List, and lots of adoring fans.

There really isn't a SECRET, just things you can do to maximize the chances of getting published, and after you're published, effectively reaching the people who will like your books. I've been doing this for so long, in my own hit-or-miss fashion, that writing itself seems old hat to me.

It's just something that gets done, between the dishes and tripping over the cats and trying to keep the laundry pile at bay. Writing is a priority, like feeding the kids, so it gets done.

If there is a SECRET, part of it hinges on that: priority.

Writing must be an absolute priority if you expect to get published. Too many people who call themselves writers don't make time for it on a daily basis. They say, "as soon as _____ (i.e., the important stuff) gets done, I'll have time to write." Wrong. **You will never *have time* to write. One must always MAKE time to write.** That is a small but crucial difference, and one reason why I tell my writing students to get a cheap kitchen timer. Even setting the timer for ten minutes a day for writing begins to shift your priorities a little bit to *include* writing.

Another part of the SECRET (if there is one) is **brute production**. You cannot just sit on one manuscript and expect the world to beat a path to your door.

Finishing a novel or a piece is wonderful, and you should definitely celebrate it. But after the hangover goes down a little bit, you need to get right back up on the horse and start something else. Don't try resting on your laurels—they wilt awful quickly.

Then there's **professionalism**, which is a part of the nonexistent SECRET. Professionalism includes:

- Reading the submissions guidelines and following them. If it says 10.5 point and double-spaced, by God, that is what your manuscript should look like.
- Saying "please" and "thank you", even when an agent or editor gives you bad news
- Understanding your editor just wants to make the story better
- Avoiding the hard sell

- Scheduling your work so you don't get avalanched and have to turn in something of lesser quality
- Learning how to take criticism

That last deserves further explication.

Writing is hard, and it's personal. There are going to be people who read your stuff who are going to be mean, rude, nasty, or just not like it. There's going to be fellow authors who knock you and reviewers who are either jealous or just don't get set on fire by your work. That's okay. Learn how to ignore that.

But **you cannot let "learning to ignore" translate out into an inability to take even constructive criticism**. A certain big-name author, a few years back, wrote in a rant about how she had worked very hard to get to a place where she never had to let an editor touch her stuff ever again. I physically cringed when I read that, because no matter how good a writer gets, **s/he is still too close to the work to effectively, professionally polish it**. You literally cannot view your own work objectively enough, that's why editors are around.

Editors and publishers are not merely distribution networks. They are a form of *quality control*, and the writer who cannot take an editor's honest constructive criticism is a writer who has already opened his or her arms to artistic death and irrelevance. Not to mention thrown their career in the toilet, in one way or another.

That's another part of the nonexistent SECRET—reminding oneself not to get wrapped up in one's own purple, turgid prose. Of course you can love your work—that's why it's yours, and that's why you're writing what you're writing—but part of love is realizing when you're not the best person to prune the work.

Incidentally, I struggle with this *a lot*. When I get an edit letter, the first thing I do is read it and literally weep. I scream, I curse, I rant, I throw pages across the room. I think I'm entitled—this is someone telling me my baby, the book I worked so hard on, isn't perfect. It isn't even close. It has warts and ugly bits. The weeping, I think, is a perfectly reasonable reaction. But then I put the edit letter aside for a week—this is time, by the way, that I insist be scheduled into the editing process—before I go back to it. And what do you know, when I go back, I start seeing the editor's point of view. "Huh," I say. "That's true, I suppose that is a horrible plot hole. Hmm. I suppose that doesn't make sense, and it would work better this way. Oh, yeah, that's inconsistent. Hrm. Guess (editor's name) is right. Well, this isn't so bad. I can live with this."

That, right there, is part of the SECRET (if it exists). Doing whatever you have to do, to **get to the place where you can take that constructive criticism** and put it to good use. The work is better for it, and it might even make one a better person (though my jury is still out on that score).

The second-to-last thing I want to mention is marketing. Yes, there is marketing involved in this biz. If you have a web presence, you need to first realize that as a public person you can't engage in some of the, ahem, less *adult* behavior people engage in on the internet. For any marketing in general, you need to get used to disappointment. There are companies that spend billions on marketing and promotion. One little writer isn't going to be able to match that investment of time and money.

On the one hand, a little bit of marketing is necessary, and **you need to think about your "brand" and your public presence**, if only to save yourself grief when your career starts to grow. On the other hand, **you need to not get wrapped around the axle when nobody notices** your marketing ploys, or when your freebies get snatched, dumped into bags, and forgotten. Such is life.

Marketing should never take more than a little bit of your time—it's easy to think things will be better if you just promote a little more. *Danger, Will Robinson! Danger!* We've all seen them, the "writers" who show up with mountains of promo material or who haunt author/promo loops, usually for small presses, whose time seems exclusively taken up with marketing. One wonders when they find time to write or refine their craft, they spend so much time flogging away at giveaways and chats and what-have-you.

The same could be said of "writers" who post constantly to their blogs—I'm not talking about the once-a-day posters, but the people who give out long posts five or six times a day, seven days a week. I always wonder why they're not writing submissions-worthy pieces with all that time.

I heard a general rule a while ago from a very good writer friend: for every six hours you spend writing, you are allowed a half-hour of promo. Promo is a *small* professional component of the job of being a writer. **Your primary job is to write**—to refine your craft and to produce. The ersatz sense of accomplishment one gets from promotions and marketing is nice, but it doesn't make one a better writer. It's just running in place mistaken for an actual journey.

This is turning into another monster post, isn't it? I should quit while the quittin's good, as my grandfather used to say. But one more thing before I go. Just one.

If there is a SECRET, there is also one deep dark component to it. **Have some fun**. Write what you love to write, write what makes you excited. If you get bored or end up with a hate-filled ulcer, there's really no point in it. If you are excited about what you're writing, if you love it, that enthusiasm will show. It will help you take the rejection, the editing, and the nasty reviews. That deep-down welling of joy even manages to make up for the non-pay, the long hours, the beating of one's head against a wall of plot and characterization. At least most of the time. *wink*

The rest of the time, dear fellow wordsmith, you're on your own.

Combat Scenes

August 8, 2008

Now, for zee fussing and zee fighting. That's right, this week my subject is...combat scenes.

I get a lot of people asking me about writing them. What advice I can give is probably not very helpful, since I don't know any more about them than the next writer. But here, let's give it a whack. Heh.

Have you ever been punched? Really punched by someone who intends to do you harm? I'm not saying you should go out and pick a fight, but the number one trouble I see with so-so combat scenes is that *they don't hurt enough*. You can tell the author has never been held down, or sucker-punched, or survived the explosion of chaos that is a barfight.

Getting hit *hurts*, and characters who can take a lot of punishment need to acknowledge that hurt. (This is right up with the disappearing bruises and wounds—if your character heals fast, there needs to be some tradeoff, and there needs to be a REASON for them to heal quickly.) I'm not saying you should go out and get yourself hit in the face. A little bit of self-defense training might help, if you get padding put on and have your instructor belt you a bit. But you have to get it through your head that getting hit is serious business. It hurts like hell, especially if someone means it. A combat scene isn't a happy cupcake party where people drink tea.

The next order of business is weapons. Have you ever held a sword, listened to the sound it makes as it clears the sheath? Ever fired a gun? If you live in the US, there's ranges everywhere where you can get elementary lessons in gun safety and learn what it's like to fire one.

I grew up with weapons around the house, and my grandfather gave me the best three rules of dealing with firearms: 1. **Always** treat a gun as if it's loaded. 2. Do not point a gun at anything you don't fully intend to kill. 3. See #1. See #1. And see #1 again.

Firing a gun at the range and getting some gun safety training will give any combat scene new seriousness and depth. One really doesn't appreciate the fact that these things are made only for killing until one sees them in action.

I do have katanas around the house. I took a dress-metal katana out into the field behind our house once, while it was still a field full of haystacks and not an apartment complex. A few minutes of hacking at a haystack with just a dress-metal blade gave me a healthy respect for just what a length of killing metal can do.

In case you haven't noticed, I do advocate healthy research. If you don't want to get bloody (which, mind you, shows intelligence), you should still try to get someone to check your work. It's like a virgin writing sex scenes—sometimes you really should get someone, erm, *experienced* to check it over for you. There's a certain amount of body-knowledge necessary to write about these things, I think.

Note that I am not saying you should go out and pick fights or get shot at. There's suffering for your art, and then there's being an idiot. I advocate the former within (tongue-in-cheek) reason and the latter (seriously) not at all.

But that's not really what we're here for, is it. Let's take a look at the mechanics of writing a combat scene. It's time for a Bulleted List.

- **Pay attention to pacing**. Longer sentences and clauses slow a Reader down. Shorter sentences and clauses speed the Reader up. Run-ons can be use to speed a Reader up, but only if used with caution and care. (You have no idea how many run-ons my editors have killed.) In the zero draft this doesn't matter quite so much, but when you revise to a first draft you need to be consciously thinking of how quickly you want the Reader to go through the combat scene. If there's a Plot Point, you need to slow down just a tad, if this is meant as pure action, be sure to cut any unnecessary weight. This is, like so many things in writing, a balancing act, it gets easier with practice.

- **Watch your adjectives.** We don't have a lot of words for either pain or pleasure in the English language (compared to some others), so adjectives are our best friends—and worst enemies too. Simile and metaphor (mostly the former) are in the same boat as adjective. In draft zero, I tend to be very lean; first draft I have to add all three; second draft I have to go through and step on the head of any overly-repeated adjective, simile, metaphor. The beta reader also has to fumigate for them. Ah, well, that's what writing is about—finding *le mot juste* instead of just *le mot whatever*.

- **Does this action DO anything?** Yeah, fight scenes are cool. I could write 'em all day. But they are in the end just SCENES, and must obey the same law as other SCENES—i.e., moving the story along. Think about what the fight is meant to convey. Is it meant to underscore the hero/ine living in a dangerous world? How does it move the plot along? Does it give characterization in showing how character/s react to disaster? A combat scene must pull several pounds of weight at once within the story arc, or it's just dead tissue. Pretty dead tissue, and dead tissue you may be attached to, but dead nonetheless and bound to start stinking unless excised. Ugh. I just grossed myself out there.

- **Seduction, Act, Crisis, Release**. Yes, combat scenes are like sex scenes, mini-arcs within the greater arc of the story. They must leave the Reader feeling satisfied—unless you consciously wish the Reader to be unsatisfied for greater dramatic tension, something you should handle with care. IF your characters have a good enough relationship with the Reader, THEN you might be able to pull off the, ahem, *coitus* or *combatus interruptus*. If they don't, the Reader will be left feeling...unsatisfied. Which can cause all types of problems. The fight scene needs to *initiate, build, explode*, and *release* tension. If you don't know whether your fight scene does, deconstruct it on a big sheet of paper. Draw the arc, and then mark each part of the fight scene according to where it goes on the arc. You may find the scene is lopsided—and now you know where to fix it.

- **Movies!** Great fight scenes in movies are a writer's friend. Go ahead and watch *Kill Bill*; *Crouching Tiger, Hidden Dragon*; the *Matrix* trilogy; old kung-fu movies; Jet Li movies; anything you like. Notice the "stylized" and implied violence in older movies, look for "realistic" fight scenes, think about the stylization of current movie fight scenes. Learning to think about angle, composition, and running time of a stage or movie fight will help you put a combat scene on paper. Of course, there is the risk of your combat scenes becoming sanitized, since movie fights tend to be overwhelmingly surreal and unreal. Which is why the next thing is so important.

- **Bloody 'em up**. This is not a tea party. This is a *fight*. Someone is at risk of getting *hurt* or *killed*. There's got to be a damn good reason for the fight, but if there isn't, there needs to be a damn good reason why the character gets entangled in it. Nobody gets out of a fight unscathed. There is ALWAYS a cost, whether it's sore muscles, split skin over knuckles, or a gunshot wound. Get used to thinking about the cost of physical, violent activity. It hurts to get into a fight, it hurts in a fight (though when adrenaline is pumping you don't feel it) and it really, really fricking hurts the morning after a fight. People get bruised, cut—a head wound bleeds a lot and is messy, a punch to the gut hurts and steals all your air, getting hit in the eye stings like hell and then your eye starts puffing closed, cutting down on your vision. It ain't fun. A fight without cost is like a magical system without cost—something to be abhorred in fiction. This doesn't mean there can't be macabre humor in a fight, or that funny things can't happen. But a fight without bloodshed really doesn't happen in the real world.

- **A little realism goes a long way**. Yes, it's fiction. Yes, there are times when you want to break real-world rules to accomplish a particular goal in fiction. Be careful what rules you break, what reasons you give for breaking them, and make sure you know the real-world rules before you break them.

- **Sensory acuity**. You notice the damndest things in a fight. Part of the adrenaline jolt is hyper-acuity—the world looks very, very strange. Stop the action in your head—think of it like a still-scene in a movie. Put it on pause and really take a look at what's going on. Where is the fight taking place? You should be able to pan around the scene in your head, back it up, look closer, pan out. A little bit of practice in visualization will go a long, long way for you here. Most writers are very good at visualization. If you're not—if you're not *seeing* the fight scene in your head—don't worry. This is a skill that can, to a large degree, be learned. (But that's another blog post.) Think of it like the movie to your book, and just practice seeing it in your head.

- **This makes you tired**. The number-one response to combat is wanting to go sleep. (After, of course, one works through the adrenaline and the adrenaline crash. After a fight, people want to: run; do a play by play; get laid; and sleep.) After soldiers make it through a battle they want to lie down and rest. The sleep makes everything dreamlike, which can be a psychological saving/distancing mechanism. I've seen this after streetfights and barfights too, and experienced it. Even after that horrid car crash I was in three Decembers ago—I got home, folded laundry (while still on the adrenaline kick) and then collapsed in bed. When I woke up, I ached in places I didn't even know I had, a familiar feeling from a lot of my misspent youth.

- **Pick every word with care**. It takes a small amount of time to read a great combat scene. It takes ten to a hundred times as long to write one. A great deal of work goes into something that will pull the Reader along in a short time. You need to pick through it with a fine-tooth comb, get rid of passivity (watch those helping verbs!) and "that"s, look for dead weight anywhere. Lean and mean is the way to do a fight scene—you can always, *always* add more later if your editor or beta needs you to. Easier to add than to trim, my dears.

- Last but not least, I keep saying it until I'm blue in the face, **make it dangerous**. Bloody your characters. If the plot is worth them getting in a fight over, it's worth getting hurt over. Beat them up. Make them work for it. Unless there is risk and cost, the Reader's heart will not leap into the Reader's mouth with fear for your fair hero/ine. That heart-in-mouth is what you *want*. Don't hesitate to put your character in harm's way. That's what great story is *about*. Or at least, what great combat scenes are about.

Go forth and bloody up some characters, dear Fellow Writer. Over and out.

Reading and the Thursday Revue

August 10, 2008

Yes, it's that time again—time for *What Is Lili Reading?* and the Thursday Revue. A word about my reviews: I tend to focus on books I really like. A book has ten pages to hook me, or I set it down. Except research reading into boring historical questions, which I normally find fascinating because I am a weirdo. Nuff said. On with the show!

First off, *Philip Kerr*. Oh, my God. Where has this author been? I am a big fan of noir. Daishell Hammett, Cornell Woolrich, and Raymond Chandler are some of my very favorite authors. There's a funky little subgenre of noir— Berlin noir—that deals with Berlin just pre-or-post-World War II. Sometimes it's shelved in mystery, sometimes in suspense, and sometimes in lit fic. And Kerr is a master of the genre. I came across an ARC of his latest (working for a bookstore does have some perks) *The One from the Other*, due out September 7th. The cover was okay, and I flipped it over to read the back. Munich? Post World War II? A private detective? All right, let's give it a shot. And damn, am I ever glad I did.

Bernie Gunther is just trying to survive in postwar Germany. He used to be a cop, and a good one—and then the Nazis came along, and everything went to hell. This is, I think, the fourth book in the Gunther series (the other three can be found in a trade paper edition from Penguin) but the exposition overload from previous books is minimal. Which means I wasn't lost, even though it's a series continuation. *The One From The Other* stands well on its own. I LOVED this book. I loved Bernie's refusal to cut himself some slack. I loved the way he didn't try to minimize the horror of the war or the Holocaust. I loved his smart mouth and the fact that he does get beaten up; he's not as young as he used to be.

We meet Bernie as he's closing down his father-in-law's hotel. His FIL is dead and Bernie's wife is in an insane asylum, catatonic. Oh, and the hotel? It's spitting distance from Dachau. Along comes an American military man who has a Nazi war prisoner, and soon they're digging in Bernie's father-in-law's hotel garden for a box of valuables stolen from Jewish victims. Bernie's digging because the Nazi war prisoner is a very sick man, and even if Bernie hates his guts he can't stand by and watch another human being be forced at gunpoint to work. Bernie's seen too much of that sort of stuff already. What with one thing and another, Bernie decides to close up the hotel and move back to Munich, where he can be closer to his wife and also earn a little money as a private detective. There are a lot of missing people in postwar Germany that someone wants found. But the cases he takes start getting more and more dangerous, and they start showing some distressing similarities. Is Bernie just paranoid, or is something dangerous and deadly going on?

Kerr writes sparely and fluidly, but it's his dialogue that really shines. One can imagine the characters speaking in German and being translated into idiomatic English. I found myself thinking of this book as Philip Marlowe in Berlin (though Bernie doesn't get to Berlin in this book) with a scar under his arm and a wolfish smile touching his face when he thinks I'm not looking. Seriously, if I had to pitch this book in one sentence it would read: *Hard-boiled noir PI with dash of "Cabaret" thrown in; add to a heavy helping of spy thriller and great dialogue. Shake, don't stir.* Yes, I know that's two sentences.

There are two problems a reader may encounter with this book. The first is that Bernie tried so hard to hold onto his own soul during the war and was only partially successful. Those who are looking for clear-cut bad guys of a certain race will be disappointed. In Bernie's world, everyone's got an angle, whether American, British, German, or Russian—or otherwise. The people you think might be the good guys are the bad guys, and even when the good guys are fighting for what they think is right they might easily be taken for bad guys. The ambiguity of good and evil in this book will give you problems if you're looking for clear-cut moral choices. The other problem is information dump. It's obvious Kerr knows his stuff, and sometimes there's a bit of wading-through-exposition that needs to be done. I will say that the history lessons are all informative and fit into the book well, representing only a temporary speedbump for me.

The only other thing that *might* be a problem for readers is the book's pace. There are so many disparate elements tied into the denouement that halfway through the book one's wondering where the hell Kerr is going—but I found myself perfectly willing to come along for the ride. And, dare I say it, half in love with Bernie Gunther, the way I'm half in love with John Dalmas and the Continental Op.

All in all, I give this book an enthusiastic thumb's up. It was so good I ordered the previous Gunther books, and I can't wait for them to arrive.

The Kiwi from LiveJournal enthused over *Freakonomics* so hard she almost popped a blood vessel, so I stole her copy and read it in one day. (Bookstore folks. We are sneaky.) It's well-written, engaging, and enjoyable. It demolishes a few sacred cows. The assertion that *Roe vs. Wade* is responsible for the (historically speaking) recent drop in crime dropped my jaw the first time I read it. The explanation of why teachers and sumo wrestlers would cheat was priceless and incidentally makes me (and other parents, I guess I'm not alone) question the WASL more than I did already. While I don't agree with some of Levitt's logic (seeing human beings as being driven exclusively by any abstract, including "incentive," is a tricky proposition at best, just take a look at Communism) I do applaud the common sense and refusal to ascribe to conventional wisdom that he espouses. (The *Freakonomics* blog is pretty sweet too.)

The book's thin, for all its densely-packed information and analysis, so I'd get it in trade paper. But it's a wonderful brain massager and very well written—more well-written, in fact, than several novels I've attempted recently. It is also a fascinating examination in the way a mind can be trained to work—discarding "convention" and looking at how people practically *act* instead of theoretically *should* act. Another thumb's up and a GeekStar award.

The Romance of Deletion

August 15, 2008

You all know how I feel about timesuck, right? Then there are those seductive things that keep us from writing, from finishing the work, and from submitting. Most of this comes from fear. And why not? This is something to be afraid of. It is an uncertain career at best, fraught from the beginning of a work to the end when the book is (hopefully) on the shelf.

Here are a few things I see young writers doing (and by "young" I mean "just starting out writing" instead of "physical age") that probably aren't helping.

Number one among those things is **romancing deletion**. I see a lot of young writers who have a WIP that they've probably written 100K words for, or something close to that. The trouble is, they've deleted 98K or so, thinking it's "false starts" or unhappy with how the work's going. They're left with the Manuscript of DOOOOOOOM, this thing that they think they'll never finish.

I've said it before: get the whole corpse on the operating table *before* you cut it up.

If a scene doesn't "work" right when you get it out, just slap its ass and leave it there as a placeholder. Chances are when you go back, you'll find out it does work after all and you were just tired, or punch-drunk, or too scared to see that it was working before.

Of course there's a *place* for deleting—I've done it myself. I made numerous false starts in the last third of *To Hell and Back*; most of those were because I had this vision of where I wanted the book to go, which wasn't where the book wanted to go. (All right, if you push me—I wanted a Traditional Happy Ending. I was close to breaking one of my cardinal rules to get one, too. Fortunately the Muse is wiser than me.) But deleting over and over again is an avoidance mechanism, and a seductive one because it *feels* like real work. It's not. If you've deleted more scenes than the work actually has in its most recent incarnation, STOP. Take a deep breath. Keep a slush file for the WIP (work in progress) where you put the bits you've chopped off. When you get stuck, go back and look at those bits. It's like a Choose Your Own Adventure.

I had trouble with two scenes in the current work (*Flesh Circus*) before I realized they actually went 20K in instead of 10K in. The Muse had just gotten ahead of herself. Saved myself a lot of work by rat-holing those scenes. Don't get sucked into the "this is a false start, I hate this scene, I better delete it." That's a good way to end up working on the same book for all of your writing life, which will be prematurely shortened as a result. You can always stop writing that scene and jump forward to the next. There's no law that says you can't go back and surgically remove a scene once the work is finished, either. Just try to ignore the siren song of timesuck so you *can* finish the work.

If you do manage to avoid this pitfall, don't worry. There are others—chief among them the ever-popular **flogging of just one manuscript**.

So you've finished a book. That's GREAT. Celebrate in whatever way you like best. Go out, get laid, get drunk, get a mocha, get a new pair of socks. Whatever (within reason) works. Then, get up the next morning and do it again. No, not the hangover-inducing part. Start working on something new—a trunk novel, something in the slush pile, a totally new WIP. It doesn't have to be *real* work—if you're anything like me, the emotional snapback between novels is immense[9]. It does feel like someone has scraped the inside of one's brain dry. But try to get into the habit of at least thinking about another work during that time, even when you're lying on the floor drooling after the immense effort of pushing the novel out into the world.

It's critical to try and stay in the habit of working even during the snapback. Don't push yourself, though—don't try to force another work out and strain your mental and emotional "muscles". Strike a balance between giving yourself enough time to recover and not getting bogged down in a slough of feeling sorry for yourself because you've worked so bloody hard.

This isn't as difficult as it sounds. The important thing is not to fall into the trap of thinking that your work is done just because you've finished a draft zero of one manuscript. It's GREAT that you've finished at least one—that already puts you in a top percentile of "writers"—but don't stop there. There's still revisions and other works to be written, especially since you have a greater chance of getting published if you submit widely.

I see a lot of "young" writers obsessing over one finished manuscript, endlessly polishing without revising, endlessly revising without submitting. Yup, you've guessed it—that's an Avoidance Mechanism. Another very, very cute and seductive one because it feels like actual work. Don't worry. There will be time and to spare for revising. There always is. It's actual creation that is the kicker, and

---

[9] Sometimes that thing you work on while in the snapback period turns into a Work in its own right, once you've recovered. That's a whole 'nother blog post.

it's the habit of healthy, sustainable creation we want to inculcate in ourselves—old hacks and young writers alike.

The last thing I see young writers doing to shoot themselves in the foot is **overplotting**. Getting so wrapped up in plotting out the world, drawing pictures of the characters, doing outlines, and role-playing that they *forget* to write.

Yes, a little bit of this is good and informs the world you're building. It makes your world and imagination much richer. But it is a thin line between this and avoiding—the seductive timesuck, again. You should never spend more time dreaming about your world than you do writing about it.

Believe me, when you're sunk in the process of writing an organic novel in a whole new world, *the world* will crawl into your head and stay there. You'll see it everywhere. You don't have to pursue it. It will hunt you down and corner you.

The joy of a creative lifestyle is just that—creating cool things for your WIP. Just mind that you work on your WIP more than you sink into the soft embrace of timesuck. I'm not saying you can't do these cool things—I am a big fan of thrift-store shopping for my characters and I also do collages for books, you have no IDEA.

But *the book comes first*. It always must come first.

Those are the biggest things I see young writers doing to spite themselves. There are other things—try out my Letter To A Young Writer—but I just hate to see beginning writers shooting themselves in the foot. It's painful to watch.

That's really all the advice I can give. My dearest younguns, you're really on your own. It's you and the keyboard (or pen and paper) and you must find your own way of wrestling it into submission. Or just enduring enough to get it all out. Good luck.

Linear or Not, The Story's Going Down

August 29, 2008

I have a subject I promised to treat—the irrepressible Fanbot from LiveJournal, this last week, asked me if I work on stories in a linear fashion, or in a non-linear fashion. (I did type "non-linearly" but my inner editor twitched and foamed at the mouth pretty hard on that one, for some effing reason.)

The answer is, it varies.

Let's assume I'm under deadline for a piece of writing. This is a good assumption because the overriding objective I have (*especially* when under deadline) is to finish the damn piece. (Please note I'm not talking about my trunk novels, or about pieces I poke at solely for my own gratification.) To that end, I generally have a daily goal of wordcount; I don't care where the words go in the story as long as I get enough of them out on a daily basis. I also do not care if those words are GOOD according to the censor in my head. At the point of sheer brute production, the point where I am creating a whole story, I don't give a damn whether they're good or not, I just care that they're there.

I should back up and explain this a little. I *do* care about producing quality work. But in the fever-heat of creation, it is so easy for the internal naysayer, that Internal Censor, to kill a work stone-cold dead or trap you in timesuck and ongoing masturbatory revision by the simple feat of saying *these words aren't good enough*. During sheer creation, quality is not my problem, it's the Muse's problem—and things go better when I leave it to that bonbon-eating bitch.

When I talk about "submission to the work", this is what I mean. You have a story to tell, you just have to get it out. You can fix technical burps and fiddles later, but you absolutely must have a whole corpse of raw footage before you can edit it into a reasonable work of art. That's why it's called a "work" of art.

Now (bringing us back to the subject at hand) sometimes the work decides it's not going to come out in a linear fashion. Sometimes the ending comes first or there's false starts, I have to do the middle and build the story around one scene (like *smoke*, actually, which started with the vision of Rose looking into the alley and combat boots twitching from behind a dumpster).

Most of the time the book starts with the hook, like Dante Valentine's very first whispered line (*My working relationship with Lucifer started on a rainy Tuesday.*). Sometimes it's the end I get first, like the crucifixion scene in *mirror* or the words exchanged between Dante and Lucifer at the very end of *To Hell and Back* (*"Here I stand, Lucifer, and not all the hosts of Hell shall move me"*/ *"Not all the hosts of Hell are necessary, Necromance. Just one."*).

When that happens, it's horrible for a pantser. Yes, I am a pantser. I write by the seat of my pants. I am not a plotter; a plotter has an outline for the book. (Note, this is a *continuum*; writers fall in varying points along the continuum. I tend to fall near the pantser end. This is not a value judgment, it's just an observation.) There is nothing as freaked-out as a pantser who has to trust that all these disparate chunks of text will somehow turn into a coherent book. If I do indeed have an ulcer, I am sure worrying about the chunks of steaming text I have to fit together is a small but significant part of its inception.

I talk sometimes about "submission to the work" (especially when I have had one too many glasses of wine and get misty-eyed). Strictly put, it is my job to show up each day, every day, and be ready to do the damn work. It is the Muse's job to provide the story and the thematic elements; at the point where I am writing the zero draft, it is not my problem to worry about whether or not the story is Good Enough. When I have the whole zero draft, *then* I can start worrying about Good Enough.

A funny thing happens—when I submit to the story and let the Muse worry about the goddamn quality control during the heat of creation, I go back to that draft weeks later when my eye is fresh and I find stuff I didn't even know I'd written. Herein lies the miracle of creativity: Most of that stuff is actually okay, if not pretty good. I find the story hangs together in a coherent fashion (most of the time). Sure, there's defects, both large (structural) and cosmetic, but those are far more easily fixed and stitched together once I have the whole corpse. I can even get you a brand-new ending (my editor for the Valentine series can vouch for this) and tweak the entire level of darkness in a book with relative ease—once I have the whole frocking book out.

It took me a long time to get to the point where I could tell myself not to care about quality while I was creating[10]. Because while you're creating, worrying about "quality" is just another way of giving the Internal Censor *carte blanche* to eff you up big time. At the point of actually getting the zero draft out there, don't worry about whether or not it's a good story. Just worry about getting the goddamn thing out of your head and onto the paper. As

---

[10] Note that I am still not fully there. It is a process, and one you never get to the end of.

Stephen King had a character say in IT[11], *it might be a terrible novel, but it will no longer be a terrible* **unfinished** *novel.*

But I'm drifting again. I do a lot of the work of plotting inside my head, and I work on whatever scene is "hot"—the one I'm "seeing" most clearly inside my noggin at the moment. Sometime the book builds itself from the beginning to the middle and then on to the end, but more often it doesn't.

For example, the current Jill Kismet book is leapfrogging itself in time as thematic elements assemble themselves, and I am still struggling with just getting the work out there and not going back and deleting while I work. (See? Even after eighteen books published and twelve or so unpublished, I STILL struggle with this. It never gets easier, the problems just get more interesting and stubborn.) Either way of working on a piece is fine, as long as I'm making progress toward getting the damn thing done. The daily goal of wordcount helps me with that.

I know a lot of people say, "But focusing on wordcount just creates more stress! It actually blocks me/scares me/makes me avoid writing." To which I reply, *honey, if that goal scares you, maybe you should find another career.*

I know a lot of people don't agree with my "do it every day" ethos, but I'm looking at this problem as someone whose money for rent and my kids' groceries largely depends on me producing work with reasonable efficiency and quality.

Once one reaches a certain point of practice and technique, the quality is there—it's hard NOT to get better if you keep writing and listening to your editors/beta readers/readers. But you have got to produce before you have any chance of getting better—really, it's like sex. You

---

[11] Which has an amazing number of little tidbits about the creative process in it, by the way.

stand a vastly better chance of getting some and getting good if you freakin' show up in the first place.

Consistently showing up on the page in the first place is critical to any kind of getting better.

My advice to the writers who ask me whether the order you write the story in matters is...don't worry about that, just worry about the story getting written. Any road you use to get there in a reasonable amount of time is fine. At the risk of trotting out a hackneyed cliché, there is no right way to write a novel. There is only the right way of writing this particular novel, and finding that way can be a matter of trained instinct, dumb luck, or trial-and-error. Let the Muse worry about the order, the thematic bits, the quality control, and the story itself.

That bitch needs to earn those bonbons, dammit.

A Few Things

September 3, 2008

Dear Readers, you are smarter than me.

Several of you have caught that Glocks don't have hammers. Yes, this is true. In my defense, I thought in a world with Weres, scurf, and hellbreed, a slightly-altered gun design wouldn't be the hardest thing for the Reader to accept. I thought other problems were bigger.

I was wrong, wrong, wrong.

I wanted a hammer for dramatic effect, Jill wanted a Glock because she likes them. I struck a bargain. I'm only glad it wasn't with Perry. *grin* I just wanted to tell you guys that yes, you're smarter than me. But you deserve to know I'm not a *total* idiot. Timeline issues and picking the wrong word in That One Notable Instance? Oh yeah, that was all me. Especially the occasional timeline burp in *Hunter's Prayer*, because I wrote that book first and *Night Shift* afterward. I'll own that.

Another thing people are writing to me about in great numbers is "why does Dante believe Eve in *Saint City Sinners*?" I guess a few folks are reading that book now, and seeing clearly that Eve is, shall we say, a touch unreliable.

You know how you see your friend doing something, and you know it's a bad idea, and you can see so clearly where it's going to go wrong—but you can't say anything, because you've tried and your friend bit your head off, and you just want them to be happy and hope like hell it'll all turn out? Even though, probably, it won't? All you can do is worry and hope? I felt that way with Dante. A LOT.

Part of the trouble with writing in first-person is you have this tight focus. You have to pull off the hat-trick of showing the reader without showing the character. Maybe I succeeded with Eve. *preens slightly* Or maybe not, since Readers are frustrated Dante doesn't twig to Eve's basic nature.

Part of the arc of the Valentine series was this deconstruction of Dante's personality. Because she is so stubborn and so dead set on what she wants and how she thinks the world is, I literally had to take her apart and destroy her before she'd listen to reason. She was such an extreme personality (I am reminded of what Janet Fitch said about the character of Ingrid in *White Oleander*) I perhaps erred on the side of wanting the reader to understand her.

Of course, that extremity of character is partly why Japh falls in love with her, and partly why she can put up with his lying, manipulative demon self, so I suppose there's tradeoffs. There always are.

Twilight, or, The Sparkly Alpha Mormon Vampire

September 4, 2008

Good morning, everyone. I have news: pump-driven espresso makers are a little louder than steam-driven ones. But they do make a lovely cup, with nice *crema*. And what happened to my old steam-driven one, you might ask? Don't ask. Please. Just let's call it "the poor thing gave its all for years and finally, gave up the ghost." While almost giving me a heart attack, I might add.

I did read *Twilight* recently, and lots of people have asked me for my opinion. I think I might best give it by giving this link[12]—Smart Bitches Sarah, on Edward Cullen as a standard romance alpha hero. For what it's worth, I completely agree. I feel profoundly conflicted about the alpha hero anyway, even when I write him.

I did go and do a *Breaking Dawn* event recently for the release of the fourth book in the series, but that was because I was asked and I like doing release events (even if they're not my book, kaff kaff). I was amazed at the energy of the mostly young and mostly female fans; but I held off reading the books because, you know, I'm writing YA too

---

[12] http://smartbitchestrashybooks.com/blog/what-is-it-about-edward/

and I didn't want to contaminate the well, so to speak. It took Cleolinda's blow-by-blow of *Breaking Dawn*[13] to convince me perhaps, maybe, I should just read this and see what all the fuss is about, contamination or no.

I picked up *Twilight* this last weekend and finished it in a couple days, in between laundry and writing and other stuff (like eating). It was a hard slog.

Meyer's obviously onto something. Her fans are legion and very excited, and the Readers, of course, always know best. But I had a couple problems with the book, most of which spring from being an adult reading a YA book and others that spring from external influences.

Let's take the external influences first. Stephenie Meyer is a Mormon[14], and my feelings about that corporation are, shall we say, less than charitable. Don't get me wrong—I would fight to the death for their right to lawfully follow the religion of their choice, and I feed all the Mormon kids who come to my door on mission. (That's part of my own vows, thankyouverymuch.)

But I had the bad fortune to read Orson Scott Card's panegyric to Meyer[15] (in *Time* magazine) right after I read his horrid little jerkwad anti-gay-marriage screed, and the two became uneasily conflated in my brain. Not to mention I've been following Warren Jeffs and the other branches of the FLDS through the news for years now, and am sickened and disgusted both by the child abuse, murder, spousal abuse, and polygyny; AND by the mainstream LDS church's refusal to both give some of its billions (raked in through tithes and things like Deseret) to

[13] http://cleolinda.livejournal.com/630150.html
[14] I am fully aware my own religious preferences, stated openly, have driven some Readers away too. That's a chance one takes with being a public personality, and a choice I made when I sold my first books dealing with the material I deal with. 'Nuff said.
[15] http://content.time.com/time/specials/2007/article/0,28804,173 3748_1733752_1736282,00.html

help the victims of the FLDS **OR** to speak out loudly against the abuses perpetrated by their fanatical co-religionists.

Knowing that about the author did color my perception of the book, and I'll admit that openly. *Mea culpa*; but I was willing to give it a chance.

However, (and here's where we get to the nitty-gritty) this is not a book I'd ever recommend to my daughter. We have a reach-and-read-it policy in our household. "If you can *reach it*, you can *read it*, and if you cannot reach it, get a stool!" I am not in the habit of censoring books for my children. If I find something objectionable, I discuss it with the child reading it. We talk about how I feel, how the kid feels about it, and the kid is free to read it as long as we've discussed it. That's reasonable, and if my daughter finds *Twilight* on the shelf and wants to read, more power to her.

But you bet your sweet bippy I'm not going to recommend it, and if she find it and wants to read it, we're going to have a talk about how your life does NOT need to revolve around some boy. Especially some boy who stalks you, tries to control your life, and sucks blood/energy. (I find the bloodsucking to be a big metaphor, but we all knew that.)

That's the crux of my problem with this book. Is Bella an appropriate role model for young women? I know you might remark, "Would you even care if you didn't know the author's religious choice?" That's a fair question, and I don't know. I do know the religious bent of the author, and the Mormon church's dismal record when it comes to female rights or even emancipation (this is still a church that educates women only in order to make them better housewives, as a friend of mine so memorably remarked not too long ago), SQUICKS ME RIGHT OUT when added to Bella's absolute inability to say no or even to enforce her own boundaries when it comes to Edward. And Edward's violation of Bella's boundaries added to his refusal to stop when she does tell him "no" because "he knows best"? Ugh. No thank you.

I have less of this problem when reading alpha-hero romance intended for an adult audience, and I can really see the attraction of Edward Cullen for teenage girls. It's great to think there is someone out there—someone handsome, brave, sparkly, "ethical"[16], smart, rich, and fantastic in all senses of the word—who will find your klutziness engaging, who will be head over heels with just *you* as a person. Believe me, I'm thirty-two frocking years old and I *still* see the attraction. But that does not mean I would ever give up pieces of myself and let someone trespass over my boundaries and take over my life ever again.

I say "ever again" because I've been there. I've been in abusive relationships and I've been stalked, and some (okay, *most*) of Edward's behavior skeezes me out to the max. I know it's supposed to be *Romeo and Juliet*-esque, and believe me I have my problems with that play too, nevermind that it was my favorite childhood Shakespeare I can still quote by the ream. (I like to think my choice of *Richard III* now shows a certain maturity. Or maybe not. *snerk*)

What really skeezes me is Bella thinks Edward's behavior is appropriate and downright fuzzy romantic, and the author placed her parents in the book as nonentities. The book could just as easily be titled "Edward Saves Bella From Absent Father And Flighty Mother, Ushering Her Into Teh Perfekt Nuklear Fam, In Which It Is Okay To Suck Blood Because Our Wimmins Are In Their Place And Everyone Is Sporty/Pretty And Camps A Lot." Which, when added to the image of a perfect family noised

---

[16] Much is made of the Cullens' ethics, as in not hunting humans. When conflated with Edward's controlling behavior toward Bella, the cognitive dissonance is jarring.

about by the Mormon church, just sends me into twitching spasms.

The fact that I know where the series ends up—with a teen marriage and pregnancy, Bella not going to college because she "wants to be with Edward so much" etc., turns me RIGHT OFF. This begs the question of whether or not I think some other aimed-at-teen-girl series are appropriate role models for young women. Like, say, *Gossip Girl* or even the American Girls series (on the younger end). I'm not speaking to those because the phenomena isn't as huge and widespread. The *Twilight* thing is, to me, a perfect storm. I cannot separate the fame of the series from my feelings about the author's possible agenda or from my feelings about the book, and knowing the series ends up with the protagonist getting hitched and knocked up instead of going to college because of a hormonal glow of first love just makes me cringe.

Edward's behavior in book one—he even STAYS THE WHOLE NIGHT IN HER ROOM when her dad doesn't know about it—and Meyer's subtle comment on the parenting styles of Bella's mum and dad just make me so uncomfortable. And opening up the book with a heavy-handed quote from Genesis about the Tree of Knowledge? Man, I was probably lost the moment I read *that*, to be absolutely honest.

I do know I'm not going to be buying/reading the rest of the series unless my daughter finds the first one on her own, reads it, and falls utterly in love. Then I'm going to have to, and I'm going to have to discuss them with my little girl. Which will be all flavors of fun for her, I'm sure. I can just see her now. "Mom, it's a *book*. I know this isn't real. It's just fun to read. Sheesh!" Which is probably the best reaction she could have.

I wish Ms. Meyer all the best—publishing being what it is, we will probably cross paths sometime in the future, and she seems like a cool person. She's made a lot of

Readers very happy, and that's awesome. I respect the hell out of that, and will probably go see the *Twilight* movie when it comes out. I suspect I will be the median age in the audience, too, given the size of the adult *Twilight* fanbase.

I'm even going to go so far as to say I read something way outside my comfort level, and I'm glad about that. Not only am I glad, but I'm happy to see the books being discussed and analyzed by people like the SBs. This just underscores the power of fiction to bring people to the table and give them a chance to talk about all sorts of things—gender roles, religion, equal rights, social expectations—without getting into a war over it.

Or at least, let's hope.

The Physical Act of Writing

September 5, 2008

I was on the treadmill this morning, and I started thinking about the physical act of writing.

Let me back up a second. I started an exercise regimen on Labor Day. Mostly because I am sick of my mother's voice in my head telling me I'm ugly and ruining my body, and partly because I have let myself go a bit. I want to be healthy and fit. I want to be able to keep up with my kids and live to a ripe old age to see what they do next. (They are *interesting* little buggers.) I've got that treadmill in the sunroom, why not use it?

I've been exercising. About a half-hour on the treadmill and a longer walk at night at the track, just to get me moving, gauge my current level, and give me a base to start from. The funniest thing happened.

My wordcount started going up.

I feel like an idiot, because I knew this about myself—I think best when I'm moving, and I plot way better when I'm up and moving around. The track near my house has seen many, many late-night sessions with me walking in circles, a knotty problem revolving inside my head and finally working itself out. Plus, when I exercise I feel better and the work doesn't seem like such an uphill slog.

It all got me started thinking about the very physical act writing is. There's the brute work of typing a novel, of course. That's sixty (YA/novella) to a hundred thousand (or more) in the finished work alone, and that doesn't count drafts, excised bits, false starts, or anything else. It's a lot of words, and a lot of work for the fine muscles and structures of the wrist and hand, not to mention the forearm.

Then there's some things that don't get counted—research, and mind over matter. I often tell people they need to swing a weapon around or actually fire a gun if they truly want to fix their combat scenes. There's nothing like kinesthetic learning to give your craft that ring of truth. The physical cost of research can be tremendous—I'll just leave that to your imagination.

Which leads us to the second thing: mind over matter. There was a story I read somewhere about a guy in prison, who spent all the time playing golf in his head, refining his swing. When he got out, he found his game had gotten so much better it wasn't even funny.

Visualization is used by athletes and in therapy, not to mention martial arts and education; it's a powerful, powerful tool. Why don't writers talk more about it? We spend hours visualizing things and putting them together for our characters. I know a lot of writers who have, for example, chronic fatigue or autoimmune disorders. One writer I know has Crohn's disease, another has lupus. For these writers, sinking into a story can be a pain-management mechanism—another one of the time-honored benefits of visualization. Sometimes the story can pull you away from real physical pain, or you can make the story hold the pain instead of your body. I firmly believe this is a GOOD thing. Hey, whatever gets you through the night, the pain, or the hellish experience is good. (There's a fine line to walk between drugging yourself with fiction and taking care of yourself, though—which is outside the scope of this little essay here. Hey, you wouldn't be reading this if you didn't expect me to digress at some point.)

Visualization is an awesome skill to have as a writer, but there's also a cost. I don't know how many times I've gotten stressed out over the story, or felt a character's physical reaction to violence or pain in my own body[17]. The cortisol and adrenaline starts to flow, because I'm not just writing the story, I'm *experiencing* it. This is good for immediacy in the work, but hard on my old *corpus*. Exercise helps purge some of that stress hormone backwash; strenuous exercise gives me a way to disconnect from the story for a few minutes and purge it. It also helps me handle the brute work of sitting down and writing better, evens out my temper, and detoxes me on a physical and mental level.

We think of writing as a sedentary (and solitary) pursuit, and to a large degree that's true. But even such a sedentary pursuit takes a toll on the body, just like a solitary pursuit such as writing has its social aspects. The toll can come from typing (Back, demon of carpal tunnel syndrome! Back!) or from stressing out over rejection, or the stress of a character's woes, or from the cost of sitting for eight hours without even a bathroom break because you're so *into* the story. (I've done that. It's not comfortable. Then there's the forgetting-to-eat thing. Ugh.)

I like to encourage writers to take care of their bodies. Even something so simple as deep breathing for five or ten minutes a day can help de-stress you and make it easier for your body to tolerate the demands placed on it by writing.

Exercise is a good thing (ritual disclaimer: talk to your doctor, don't overdo it, better to start small and get into a habit than weekend-warrior it and break something, etc., &c.). Just because you "just sit and write" doesn't mean

---

[17] Interesting side note: I should mention that reading *Somatic Fictions* before bed has given me a new grasp on the whole subject. If literary criticism and analysis is up your alley, check it out.

there's not a cost to your physical and mental systems. Helping to minimize that cost means you can write longer.

It also means you have a better chance of writing higher-quality stuff. A longer professional life and healthier body means more chances to overcome the constant round of rejection that is a writer's life, and more chances to produce something that will eventually sell.

Think of taking care of your body as a necessary investment in your writing life. It's not the only reason to exercise, but sometimes it's the only reason I can drag myself through another round.

When all else fails, I can whip myself with plot and characterization. Hey, man. Whatever works.

Young Jedi, You Must Do

September 12, 2008

Come sit at the feet of Auntie Lili, dear Readers. I'm sitting here with sweat drying on me from the treadmill, having my morning cup of coffee, and feeling just the teensiest bit ornery. Let's talk about something writerly. Let's talk about the *I could do it betters*.

Before we get into this, a public service announcement. If you don't agree with me about writing or about the creative process, fine. Go read someone you do agree with. Don't send me hate mail or comment about how you're a precious speshul snowflake and I've destroyed your will to write/live. Any and all such comments/hatemails will be ruthlessly mocked and bashed on the head. My patience, she has officially been exhausted. Besides, if my teensy little opinion can wreak such terrible damage on you, you are low-lying fruit and would be offended/damaged by any old thing; you just happened to choose my stupid little opinion. Get over yourself.

Ahem. Sorry. That just fell out. I now return you to your regularly scheduled Lili.

I'm reading a few different books right now. *Ivanhoe* with the Selkie, taking Kage Baker's *Mendoza in Hollywood* in little chunks on the treadmill because I want it to LAST, Cormac McCarthy at the kitchen table, and Jane Smiley by my chair. Despite this (and the huge TBR pile), I have trouble finding books I like.

When one writes for a living, reading for pleasure becomes a much chancier proposition, because one gets terribly picky. You're always peering under the hood, so to speak, wondering why the author made *this* choice instead of *that* choice; picking apart the sentence structure, anticipating twists, poking little holes in motivation and plot. I would hazard that professional musicians do much the same. It's hard to turn off the automatic editing inside one's head, and *really* hard to find a book that carries one along with it so strongly the editor is drowned out and the temptation to look under the hood doesn't get a chance to surface.

That's one reason for the *I could do betters*. Another is a young artist just starting out, growing out of the fanfic phase and feeling the constraint of other people's characters. It always starts with the same thought. *Hey, that's a neat idea...but it would be even neater if the author did x,y,z...You know, I'd do it differently. I'd set it up THIS way.* The less-charitable version of this thought: *Holy fuck, that's CRAP*. **I could do better than this.**

And lo, a prime source of motivation is uncovered.

It's kind of déclassé to admit you want to do something better, or that you've made a value judgment about someone else's book and want to "do it right". Most writers will never, ever admit they think this—as indeed, any reasonable human being would hesitate to. Wild horses won't drag it out of them, nor will wild horses drag out *which* books they've thought this about. (That is a subject reserved for close friends and alcoholic lubrication, if the conversation in the bar at several conventions is any indication.)

This is a good thing, actually. Be careful who you open your mouth about the *I could do betters* to. You never know who might be listening and, publishing being the close little business it is, that person could have control of the next stage of your career at some point. In other words, *think* this all you want, but be careful who you *say* it to.

Still, it's a motivation. And if it gets you writing your own stuff, it's a valuable source and shouldn't be discounted. It's a sign you're starting to read critically instead of just instinctively—by which I mean you have internalized some of the rules of good writing/storytelling, and the internalization of those rules means you will start making a better class of writing mistakes. Hey, the mistakes don't ever go away. You just make new ones as you get better.

Unfortunately, for every motivation, there is a dark side. The dark side of this motivation blooms to its noxious excess in the Holier-Than-Thou Fan and the I'm Gonna Writer.

The Holier-Than-Thou Fan is that "blocked" writer who continuously sniffs that Such-And-Such Author is *all right,* they guess, but would be *so* much better if they did X. The HTTF will give this advice to a writer from the vast heights of their disinterested condescension, usually in the most hurtful, sneering manner possible. When questioned about their own work, the HTTF will airily remark of *course* they're writing, but the world isn't ready for their (unfinished) heartbreaking work of staggering genius yet.

Besides, they're Such-And-Such Author's *biggest* fan, and they're *just* trying to help! They're too busy fucking tearing down actual working authors/artists to finish their own goddamn work, and they get their jollies from the passive-aggressive *But I'm just trying to help you! You'd be such a pretty girl/good artist if you lost some weight/did what I told you!*

Avoid these like the plague, dear fellow writers. Thank them for their input and go on your way. You will never be able to satisfy them, and if you don't engage they cannot insert their proboscis under your tender skin and suck the ruby fluid beneath.

The I'm Gonna Writer is a different animal, one that hunts in critique groups, writer's gatherings, and conventions. The GW is *gonna*. Gonna finish that huge work, gonna blow the socks off everyone, gonna wow the world, gonna gonna gonna...but they never do, and they won't take crit. The Gonna Writer knocks other authors with abandon, far more directly than the passive-aggressive HTTF. The Gonna Writer won't show you the manuscript, because s/he's had problems with people "stealing" their work. The Gonna Writer is not going to finish a single goddamn thing.

And Heaven help you if you have to provide crit for him or her. You may get a peek at their mess of a manuscript, but when you try to offer constructive pointers, all of a sudden you are The Enemy. Your advice will be scoffed at, and the GW will suddenly flood you with thousands of Reasons. Reasons why you've misread the work, reasons why it *has* to be the way they're writing it, refined and urbane allusions they're making that are leagues beyond what any uninitiated hack can speak to. In other words, they're not going to listen to a goddamn thing you say.

Both the HTTF and the GW are engaging in that most seductive of timesucks—endlessly talking instead of sitting down and doing. Talking endlessly about how great the work is going to be is much more romantic and gets more positive strokes than the thankless slogging of doing the damn work every day.

This brings us (somewhat circuitously, but hey, you know I digress and this is my journal, it's allowed) to the point. **All the "I could do better" in the world is useless without hard work.**

Young Jedi, it is perfectly okay to feel this way about your reading material. I would go so far as to say it's a natural recurring phase in a writer's life. Use that feeling to get yourself to the keyboard each day. Use it to help you flog yourself through the finish line. Use it to help yourself. Don't give other people the benefit of this opinion—it is meant to be a spur to three people: you, yourself, and yours truly.

Of course, if you're dishing with your best friend and a cranky, catty comment slips out, well, who can help that? It's what dishing and best friends are for. Just, for God's sake, be sure you can trust the friend you dish with. Like any source of motivation, the *I could do betters* have their dark side, and they are useless without the commitment to actual work. It doesn't matter where you find the motivation—anywhere will do, my ducks. Take it where you find it.

But trying, or just thinking *I could*, isn't enough. There is do, or do not. It ain't romantic and it ain't pretty, but it is the bottom line, and it will get you published faster than the Perpetually Unfinished Manuscript Of Staggering Genius will.

Always An Explanation

September 15, 2008

To be a writer is to be an inveterate observer.

Yes, the world will roll in ecstasy at your feet, even without your effort. But writers are dyed in the wool voyeurs, and if they don't start out that way the search for material will make them so.

It's not that you have to look very hard for stories. They are hanging from the vines all around you. I went out for Thai last night, all alone. It's not often I get out alone, though I had Teresa Mendoza for company (I LOVE *Queen of the South*, reread the whole damn thing in one gulp yesterday). As I was sitting there, turning pages and waiting for my Pad Kee Mow—I love that dish, and not just because the phrase "drunkard's noodles" makes me giggle—a story unreeled in one of the other booths.

She was beautiful, in a freckled, healthy way. The type of girl with long brown glossy hair, a clear misty complexion even with the freckles. She had that upper-middle-class all her life look, little gold ball earrings, expensive but not designer clothes. A type of well-bred innocence. A tilted up cheerleader's nose.

He was another tale entirely. Heavy now, but you could see he'd been on the football team in high school. Round face, dark buzzcut, scruffy beard that would have looked raffishly engaging minus a few years and about fifty pounds. A T-shirt that had seen better days, and shorts that strained at the waist and fell to the knee. Hairy legs. Sandals that were popular last year.

I pegged them as long-term boyfriend and girlfriend, probably two years out of high school, him struggling to make it in a world where he didn't have the school-hall ecology to make him a big predator. *She's going to leave him behind in a little while, unless she gets knocked up*, I thought. Hey, I'm allowed to think what I want.

I settled down with my book and the waiter who knows me took my order and left me alone. Then I noticed the girl was holding her hands out cupped on the table, and he wouldn't touch her. It was a strangely supplicating gesture on her part.

My nose for plot tingled.

"It's not just that you lie," she said finally. "It's that you always have a *reason*." My ears perked. He said nothing. She moved her hands back, but he was quicker, dropping his fingers into hers. A shadow of distaste crossed her face, but she left her arms stretched out the way they were.

I took this in, little sips of glances over the top of my book. They were so busy with each other they didn't notice me, and I've learned the trick of un-obnoxious surveillance.

"Baby—" he finally said. Pleading, a sort of nagging tone. I'd guess it had always worked before.

"No." She sat up straighter. "If you didn't always have a reason for things not matching up, I'd believe you. But you've always got a reason. You always *explain*. You haven't changed at all."

He let go of her and settled back, crossing his arms. I couldn't see his face, but his entire body shouted. I had to watch the reflection in her body language to figure out *what* it was shouting, though.

She took a sip of her water, folded her hands in her lap. They were silent. My noodles came. Her tomato noodle dish came about thirty seconds later. He stuck to water. I took this in and made a private bet with myself that she'd be picking up the bill. She ate with good appetite, like every bite was her last. Quick but neat, nice manners. The waitress filled up her water.

I kept my ears tuned.

"It wasn't my fault," he said suddenly. "It's a hard job. And that bastard—"

She set her fork down and fixed him with her big brown eyes. "I'm not moving back." Quiet and firm. Pushing a strand of long brown hair back behind her ear. Her earring glittered in a reflection of sunlight bouncing off a passing car's window. "You had enough money to go out drinking. You had enough money for an Xbox. You had enough money for weed."

"It's not my fault," he repeats, slouching back further.

"Was *she* not your fault too?"

"Liz[18]. Come on." Cajoling. I got the idea he'd said it a lot before. He reached his hands out, almost touching her plate.

She looked down, took another bite. I got the idea she wasn't really eating the noodles. It was some other dish she was tasting, a bitter taste but one she liked. "You always have a reason." Another bite, chewing mechanically. "I'm going back to college."

"College girl." Now he was nasty, but he tried to make it sound affectionate. "I had to work."

"Everyone's got to work." She lost her appetite, pushed her plate away. "Are you ever going to grow up?"

He shrugged. I saw the movement of one meaty shoulder. The distaste was open now, drawing down her mouth and crinkling her forehead. I saw what she was going to look like in a few years. If she went down the bitter road, she would get washed-out; if she didn't, she would

---

[18] Names changed for obvious reasons.

still be pretty. They looked at each other. More silence. I ate a little more tofu, considered the situation. Took a long draft of water. It was icy against the sting of peppers.

She finally looked away. Scooped up her Coach-knockoff purse and dug in it. "I don't know why I did this," she finally said. "What am I going to do with the cat?"

Now he leaned forward, a fisherman who senses an escape. A last desperate tug on the line. "My dad's picked the cat up, and my television. The rent's paid through the end of the month."

She laid a bill down on the table and scooted out of the booth. She moved stiffly, like an old woman. "Your dad?"

"I gave him my key. He'll turn it in at the office. The lease is up this month."

She looked down at the table and her still-steaming plate. "Have a nice life, Jay."

He stared at her. She turned and walked away. Didn't look back once as she made the hard turn at the end of the aisle. From behind my book I watched her walk out the front door and into the golden heat.

Now, that was interesting. Jay sat at the table for a few minutes, then hooked her plate across. When I glanced up next the bill she'd laid on the table had disappeared and he was halfway through her food. By the time I'd finished my noodles he was done.

The waiter stopped by to ask how things were. "Perfect as usual," I said. "How about a salad roll? And a choclatini?" I need something sweet to get the bitter out of my mouth.

"Celebrating tonight?" He gives me a gap-toothed smile. He's a nice kid.

I grin back. "Just out by myself."

"Yeah, I never see you alone. Choclatini coming up!"

"Thanks." He strides away.

I watch Jay. He thinks he's alone in this, his tragedy. I wonder what's going on inside his head, if the story's finished. This is where I would probably end if I was writing the short story. Tie everything off nice and neat.

In fiction, you can do that.

Jay slides to the end of the booth and glances around. His eyes pass over me quietly reading my book, dismiss me. He gets up. He's stockier than I first thought, and he heads for the restrooms. They're down a long hall, and he's chosen his moment well. The staff are either at the bar or on the other side of the restaurant. Jay nips smartly out the side door the waiters use for going out onto the patio. There's a few couples out there, but I'd bet money he keeps heading for the back of the building. He can walk around and get to his car that way, assuming he has a car.

The waitress for that side of the aisle comes back, looks at the empty table, and looks around for a whole twenty seconds—a long time in the restaurant trade. She says something under her breath and begins clearing the table.

My waiter comes back with the choclatini. She stops him, asks him a question in the language they share. He looks around, then his face changes to a picture of dismay. They unobtrusively scan the whole restaurant, but it's too late. She bears up well, shrugging and taking the plate. It's empty and strangely clean, scraped dry. In under two minutes the table is cleaned and reset, their water glasses—hers three-quarters full, his empty except for ice—gone. I catch sight of her talking to the manager, a stolid Asian man who shakes his head and rolls his eyes.

My waiter comes back with salad rolls. I want to ask him about it, but I keep my mouth shut. I go back to my book. Neither the manager nor the waitress look particularly surprised, and I see the manager pat her shoulder and say something obviously soothing. He shrugs, makes another comment, and their laughter rises.

The cook is in on the joke, he laughs from the other side of the steam counter too. When I'm finished, I tip double and leave.

A few years ago I might have paid her bill, hating to see a waitress taken advantage of. (What part of witnessing makes me responsible? What part of the role of observer have I chosen to escape responsibility?) Now, however, I walk out into the hammerblow heat of a ninety-degree afternoon. I drive the long way home, and when I get there I am strangely pleased to see the kids smiling and bouncing.

You see? The world offers stories everywhere. Raw material. Sometimes the writer's offended sense of symmetry will provide the ending. Sometimes all you get is a snapshot. The lives keep going on, and on, with us stealing little glances around the corner, peeking. The most private of tragedies, the smallest of crimes, played out in the most public of spaces, right under the nose of everyone.

When some people tell me they can't find story ideas anywhere, I often just stare at them, amazed. Stories are always there, ripe for the plucking. They fall out of everything. The world teems with them, crowds of unquiet ghosts just waiting for an open door to step through. All you must do is look.

The Art of Observation

September 17, 2008

The previous post brought a number of comments—thank you, everyone—and one intriguing question. Cat asked: *What's the trick to un-obnoxious observation? I'm an aspiring author and it seems to me like a good thing to learn.*

I live now in a rural area, but I spent the majority of my teens and half my adult years in an urban city environment. The kinda place where a wrong look to the wrong person could get you in big trouble real fast, especially for (at the time) a single, pretty, petite girl like I was. So I've cultivated the habit of keeping my eyes down, my thoughts to myself and just going about my business.

Even though now I live in a rural area where people are more friendly and open, I find it a hard habit to shake. I've even had friends and family feel slighted because I didn't notice them waving at me in traffic or other places, but the truth is I just didn't see them because I've trained myself not to look around.

This may be part of the reason why as a young author I find it difficult at times with characterization. I feel that un-obnoxious observation would help me in this regard. So any advice or little tricks you could give about author observation techniques would be extremely helpful.

Hm. Characterization, I firmly believe, is a stepdaughter of observation and perhaps the niece of sympathy, certainly the handmaiden of imagination. While one can't reduce characterization to observation, observation is definitely a large part of it.

Being an inveterate voyeur as a writer also carries with it the responsibility of respecting people's privacy to reasonable extents. Eavesdropping is seductive, and it can turn pathological (though I don't know how much of that pathology is the result of someone just determined to be a jerk from the beginning; but that's another blog post entirely). This is why I like to use the qualifier "un-obnoxious". To fully discuss this, I think we should start with a brief note about my childhood, therapy, and then talk about massage school, just to set the stage

It was a family truism that I "had my head in the clouds". I remember my grandfather endlessly telling me I had to wake up and pay attention to the "real world". Of course I was an imaginative child, but I always thought I was kind of heedless until my therapist told me I was actually hyperaware. She made this statement when I asked her how I could focus better and pay attention more. She noted I came into her inner office and always chose a specific seat—one that was uncomfortable, but placed so I could see the room and had an easy exit, and that I was always perched on the edge of it and watching her face and the door at once.

That was, incidentally, the point at which I started trusting her. I'd chosen that seat deliberately after a series of lightning-fast calculations "sizing up" the physical space; calculations I didn't think about because I thought everyone made them. I learned that contrary to my family's assertions, I had actually learned to pay very close attention to the emotional weather in a room, watching people's faces in sidelong glances and reacting with disproportionate caution or challenge to any hint of anger or disapproval—while always keeping an escape route in sight.

Anyway, cut to a few years earlier, when I was in massage school. Slight digression here: Yes. You do have to go to school to get certified, though it's been years since I practiced. The time I spent in massage school was fantastic, because it taught me a **LOT**—about boundaries, nonviolent dispute resolution, self-respect, the power of the mind and body. I wanted to do relaxation massage and found out I had a knack for treatment. The bodies just spoke to me, each in their own way, about how to help them heal themselves[19].

In massage school, we practiced palpation. This is the art of identifying the structures under the skin. You have to accurately identify what's under your fingers, elbows, wrists, forearms—because you can seriously hurt someone by messing about in, say, the cervical region. Or the abdomen.

Palpation was scary for each and every student. First, we were practicing on each other, so if you messed up (and the teachers scared us into caution) it was your classmate, someone you knew and saw every weekday. Then there was the whole thing about feeling stuff under the skin, which was thorny for a number of reasons.

Last but certainly not least, there was the fact that you can't feel a damn thing when you palpate for the first few thirty or fifty times. That's why studying your anatomy is so important. You have to have the mental idea of what *should* be under your touch. "Even if you can't feel it," one instructor remarked, "act like you do." She paused, eyeing us. "In other words, fake it 'til you make it, baby."

---

[19] I firmly believe that a majority of the time, the body just needs a little help to sort things out. It's not healing the body, it's helping the body heal itself. All standard disclaimers to this opinion apply, since I am not currently a medical professional.

I was scandalized. Faking something as important as this? My expression must have shown it, and the other students looked shocked as well.

"It's just the way palpation works," the instructor said, not defensively at all. Rather, she was stating a simple fact. "You have to expect to feel what's down there before you actually can. I think it's your brain sorting out new ways to pattern the stimuli, but that's just me. This way works. Trust me."

Well, we did. We had no choice. And it was the *damndest* thing. Once you faked it for a little while, straining your brain to remember the structures under the skin, at some point something clicked. It was an almost physical "click". You could see it happen to people. Their faces would light up, they would relax, and their entire posture changed.

It was the coolest thing to feel the "click" when someone was working on you. All of a sudden the touch would change. Instead of a hesitant, helpless prodding, all of a sudden the practitioner's hands would drop down into your tissue and start dancing with the things under the skin, soothing almost before you could tell them where the ache was.

For me, the click just dropped everything into place. All of a sudden the person on the table wasn't a just a collection of parts or a test or even a classmate. After that click, the instant I touched someone, *I knew* where they hurt.

I do not know whether this is a form of telepathy or the brain processing a huge amount of information in splits of split-seconds. I don't care, either. As S. Jason Black once remarked, when I put my key in the ignition and the car starts for the thousandth time, coincidence is not relevant.

Trust me, this is wending toward a point.

Observation is something kids learn early. Our entire social conditioning rests on observing how other people are feeling. (Slight note: I do realize there are people who don't. Inappropriate social behavior as a result of misreading cues or interpreting them incorrectly happens for a variety of reasons and in a variety of degrees, all of which are outside the purview of this essay. Don't use that as a red herring, mmkay?)

Where I'm going is simple. The first step toward becoming an observer is to realize you have probably been doing this all your life, and you can sharpen those skills with very little effort. The next point is this: fake it 'til you make it, baby. This is the sort of endeavor that feels goddamn awkward at first until the "click" happens. After that, good luck turning it off—but that is, also, outside the purview of this little chat.

I had not realized my hyperawareness of mood swings and likely danger in my childhood had affected my ability to observe people. I was amazed to find out other people didn't have a constant testing of the weather going on inside their heads. I was doubly amazed to find out other people didn't constantly scan for signs of the next "explosion".

My therapist gently pointed out I was always waiting for hammers that didn't fall, and when I sensed someone was upset or angry, I immediately tried to anticipate what I could do to defuse the situation, trying strategy after strategy—and if the person didn't respond in the ways I'd been conditioned to expect, I grew very nervous and fretted myself into a lather waiting for the storm.

The positive side of this, and an effect from my years as a massage therapist, was my instant sympathy with people I observed in public settings. The gift of the problem, so to speak, was that I was already a finely-tuned observer. I just had to turn that skill set toward the writing, which I did without even being aware of it. It was just like seeing someone walking by and knowing just by the way they moved that they'd had a knee injury, and then running over possible ways of treating it inside my head. Palpation will do that to you. *rolls eyes*

I sense I'm digressing and getting boring here. But a lot of what I'm about to recommend will make little sense unless I first explained the principles behind why I think these things work.

I can separate the art of un-obnoxious observation out into two parts: common courtesy and the actual skills.

Common Courtesy

I suggest observation in public places.

First of all, a brightly-lit public place is less dangerous. There is also a social compact in place in public places—as long as you are obeying the "rules of the road" you are well-nigh invisible and can watch what you want. Also, the places I recommend are usually full of people going about their business and too busy to wonder about you.

Shopping Malls: These are like museums in action. Cultural assumptions, family and social dynamics, expectations of anonymity and proper behavior, and cross-sections of society, all available, and at very low cost.

Libraries/Museums: Less traffic, but the people are often weirder. Also relatively low-cost.

Casinos/Racetracks: Really I don't recommend racetracks, but Bukowski loved them. These are higher-cost and a bad idea if you have addiction issues. They're only available for people of a certain age, but they are full of human nature on display.

Coffee shops/street cafes: These can be slightly higher-cost too, but they give the advantage of watching two spheres at once—inside the restaurant space and outside on the street.

Grocery/Convenience Stores: When you're out shopping or filling your tank, you have a golden opportunity to observe people. These differ from the above in that they're dictated by your needs and you can't loiter endlessly.

Fairs/Granges. For the rural-living, look around. Humans are endlessly social and there is bound to be some place where people hang out. I am an urban creature, and I am most familiar by now with American urban spaces. My apologies—all I can tell the rural writer is that there's bound to be somewhere people get together to chew the fat. (I leave observation of Nature for another blog post.)

These spaces are treasure troves for the writer. But you need to follow a few rules.

Stay out of the way. Malls are my first choice because you can buy a coffee or something, sit on one of the benches or in the food court, and watch for literally hours. In casinos, the expectations are different—if you're in a lounge or just wandering around, you may need to have a soft drink or something. It's your rent for being in that space. You also have to know the rules operating around gambling tables, or the casino can ask you not to come back.

Coffee shops need their tables after a reasonable amount of time, unless they're in a slow period. So do restaurants. A little courtesy toward the space itself goes a long way. I've had a lot of luck in restaurants by simply saying, "I'm going to be here a little while. If you get busy I'll move on. Is there a place I can sit and have a cup of coffee that's out of your way?" while holding up my notebook with a hopeful smile. Courtesy goes a long, long way; waiters and waitresses are more than willing to let me sit and nurse a coffee for a long time. They'll make small talk and tell me about their lives and the restaurant biz. I always make a point of tipping very well. Coffee is cheap, and the couple dollars in extra tipping buys me goodwill next time. I've even had some joints spot me the coffee because the staff enjoys the sensation of being listened to, of being important.

Don't take advantage of this—goodwill is hard-bought and easily lost. If you're asked to move on, do it. There are always other spaces.

Don't stare. Take a notebook with you and jot down sentences. If you look like you're writing, the curious will largely leave you alone. This is excellent exercise. It will also give you a reason to glance up, take in the atmosphere, study something or someone, and then glance back down.

Staring at someone in a public space can get you labeled as creepy, attract the attention of security people who have other things to look out for, or can be interpreted as a challenge. Besides, it's rude. If you are taking advantage of the social compact in a public space, you need to observe it.

Rules and Skills

Listen, listen, listen. I repeat this one because few people truly listen. They are too busy planning the next thing they're going to say inside their heads. Listening in public places will give you an ear for how people really talk—what they say, what they don't say, how tone interacts with volume and emphasis to give context. You could do far worse things than learning to listen.

Pay attention, Part I. Don't focus on horking up a masterpiece in your notebook. Rather, jot fragments. Go for the telling detail. Don't worry if it makes no sense to you later. *This* is not an exercise in writing for sense. This is Grist For The Mill. You are giving yourself a glut of stimuli so you can get to that "click". Don't stint yourself.

Pay attention, Part II. Don't do this in public parks after dark. Don't scribble in your notebook while hanging over a poker table. Don't be so involved in scribbling in your notebook you walk out in front of a car. Don't stare at the couple having a disagreement or give a dirty look to the

171

howling kid and the overstressed mother. Don't make challenging eye contact with a group of punks with nothing better to do. Exercise some caution with your own safety.

A note here: I've sometimes disobeyed my own advice, mostly when I was young and stupid and hanging out in bad, bad parts of town. I don't recommend it. Really I don't.

Detachment? There are a few different schools of thought about this. Should you be a disinterested, dispassionate observer—as far as you can be? Should you allow the cruelty and pointlessness that you may see—and believe me, you WILL see plenty—to "get to you"? Should you make judgments about what you see?

It's up to you. Write to answer those questions, if you must. But in the end, it's up to you.

Time yourself. You can get over-stimulated *really* easily. This can also become a timesuck used to distract yourself from actually writing. Set yourself a time limit and stick to it. I recommend a half-hour to start with, once a week.

The "What-If game". When I was about nine, a blinding realization struck me. Every car we passed on the freeway was inhabited by people who had *completely* different lives.

What if the guy in the red Honda was really a government spy? What if that lady in the truck was the world's greatest horse trainer but nobody knew it? What if, what if, what if?

I've never grown out of the habit. This is part of what I mean when I say "stories are lying all around." It doesn't take more than a few minutes of watching people before the what-ifs start flopping around in your head, begging for some attention.

Unobtrusive and un-obnoxious observation depends on obeying the social compact and politeness toward the space. Once you get practiced at observing people in public spaces, a funny thing happens: a part of your brain steps back and starts observing people all the time. I call this "writer brain"—the part of me constantly taking notes. It becomes a kneejerk reaction, like looking under the "hood" of a car to see what makes it work—or not work. Sometimes I wish I could turn it off. The dark side of it is that I have very few times where I simply sink into the moment and *be*.

The irony is twofold: most people have very few such times, thousands of dollars are spent on simulacra[20]; and those times when I sink into the moment most completely and just "am", I'm generally...writing. I know there is a divine presence out there somewhere, if only because of little ironies like that.

My problem is something opposite of Cat's above. My childhood hyperawareness rarely lets me observe without feeling anxious and looking for the next explosion. It's gotten better now that I have the words to describe the process and familiarity with it, and channeled it toward writing. But that was something I had to learn in massage school too—how *not* to take on a client's pain.

You can call it "boundaries" if you want, and having a tender heart or strung-tight nerves can make observation a terrifying experience—which is why I recommend timing yourself. You are engaged in not only watching other people, but watching your own responses, thoughts, judgments and the like. It is hard to stare into the mirror of humanity without seeing yourself reflected—both good and bad.

Well, I went and got philosophical and wrote a monster of a post. I'm tired now, so I think I'll bring it to a close. Cat, I hope this answers some of your question—and the question was far more complex than I think either of us realized. *eyes post* I think I went rushing in there

---

[20] To list just a few: drugs, self-help books, trend-of-the-moment "meditation" classes, video games, compulsive shopping—need I go on?

where angels fear to tread. I suppose if one's going to be a writer, a healthy dose of such rushing is probably inherent in one's makeup. The labyrinth of the human heart is not to be walked lightly.

On the other hand, I have rarely been so endlessly amused as when I've been watching the vast cavalcade and panorama of my fellow beings. I find them endlessly interesting. Which is, I suppose, why I ended up in this job...

...but that's another blog post. *wink*

On Agents

September 26, 2008

I get a lot of mail that runs like this: "*Hi Lili, love your work. Can you tell me the name of your agent? I'm an aspiring author/the author of a work named _____ and I wonder if...*"

There are two reasons anyone might send one a letter like this. The more charitable explanation is the person honestly wants some advice—they're awash in the fog of confusion that can be submitting your work. They want to know what worked for me, in my search for the Grail of Getting Published.

Since most of these letters come with attachments—samples of the work in question—I can only assume they fall into the other category. Which roughly translates out to this:

- *Hi Lili, love your work.* Translation: **Here's how I'm going to soften you up.**

- *Can you tell me the name of your agent?* Translation: **Now that I've complimented you, you owe me something.**

- *I'm an aspiring author/the author of a work named _____, and I wonder if...* Translation: **This is a sales pitch, and since you owe me, you have to spend time you could otherwise use** *writing your own stuff to take a look at mine, since I am the center of the universe.*

I'm fairly sure it isn't **meant** this way. I'm sure they have the purest intentions in the world. But as with so many things, it's not what they meant but what actually gets across that sends those emails straight to the rubbish bin.

Still, though, it's my self-chosen job in these Friday posts to tell you about the life of a working writer, and an agent is part of that life. It's a subject that could use a little demystification. As much as I can offer from my own personal experience, that is.

Let me tell you how I got an agent, and how I recommend one might go about getting one.

I got my agent through hard work.

The actual names etc. are something I can't talk about for various reasons, but I can give you a story and a thought. A friend of mine had a girl he was dating; this girl was an "author". We met for lunch because she wanted advice, and the "author" didn't really want advice—she wanted the name of my agent and an introduction. The world revolved around her, apparently, and I was just a cog in it.

I suggested she take the path I did: work like hell, submit to small presses, build relationships with small presses, then network inside those relationships until you've accumulated *bona fides*. Those *bona fides* function as entrees, and I met my agent almost accidentally—

"Oh, no," she interrupted. "There's not enough money in small press."

Right then was the point at which I signed off from the conversation.

This job pretty much pays shit, especially if you've got any prima-donna notions about being so cool and wonderful the world will of course pay your rent and groceries just-because. If you're determined not to work hard and work up because it's beneath you, nothing I say is going to help and I'm sure as hell not going to put my good name on the line recommending you to my agent. Puh-*leeze*.

Chance favors the prepared mind.

In other words, I did meet my agent almost accidentally, through the good offices of someone I knew in small-press publishing. Someone vouched for me because I was prepared—I had worked my ass off, turned in reasonably-salable product, met my deadlines, and taken my editing like a pro. I had shown I was professional and reasonable to work with, *ergo*, the person who had an amount of credibility vouched for me, and my agent read my stuff with that in mind. I didn't have to go through the slush pile, and I had *earned* a little bit of goodwill by being professional.

Goodwill does not come to you as an angel in the night to the undeserving. Goodwill needs to be earned with hard work and professionalism. This is a constant in pretty much every career, and I don't know why people think writing is different. You do hear about overnight successes or books culled from the slush pile, but these are not the typical road. It's like that little thing on weight-loss infomercials—the fine print saying *Results not typical*. Which means "Don't hold your breath, Fanny."

There are, to my mind, a few different ways to get an agent. All of them require hard work. You can: 1. Work hard, polish your craft, do your Writer's Market research and submit, submit, submit to agents. If you practice and produce and submit, sooner or later the law of averages will work in your favor and someone will want to buy your stuff. 2. Work hard, polish your craft, make friends who do the same, do your research, submit to small presses instead of agents. Build your repertoire that way, practice and produce and submit, and sooner or later the law of averages will work in your favor. 3. Other variations of the above, all with hard, consistent work in the starring role.

You can write a heartbreaking work of staggering genius that will make the world beat a path to your door. I don't entirely rule that out. But the chances of you doing that, my dears, are astronomically small. You will have better luck winning the lottery or having an airplane part fall out of the sky and onto your head. In other words...don't hold your breath.

It's possible, sure. It's possible tomorrow aliens will land and the world will be turned into Candyland. And flying monkeys might sally forth from my rectum. All these things are possible, but not **probable**. The name of this game is to make it increasingly *probable* you will get published. To do that, you have to realize you are one in a sea of thousands sending in slush.

Slush piles are monstrously huge, and your work can and will get lost in them. You might have the best book in the world, but it might get read right before lunch when an editor/agent is hungry, or pissed off, or just plain tired of reading crap. That's why it's the slush pile—there's a low, low chance your work will be: 1. read in a timely fashion (because of the huge numbers involved—these are people, not superhuman publishing machines!) 2. read while the editor/agent is concentrating fully on it 3. given more than a cursory chance.

Working on your craft and your *bona fides* does not GUARANTEE getting an agent/published. But it ups the chances by an order of magnitude. Instead of a crapshoot you've suddenly got *real* chances, and the more you polish your work, submit, learn, and have professional relationships with others in the trade, the better those chances get.

Getting an agent isn't a mystery. There are things you can do to maximize your chances. Agents want books— this is why they bother having slush piles and professional relationships with other people in the biz. They *want* authors who know their craft, are salable, and are professional. *They* are actively looking for these things.

Being these things makes it exponentially easier for an agent to take a chance on you—put their good name and credibility to work for you. This makes it easier for a junior editor to put their good name and credibility to work for you in convincing a senior editor, or a senior editor to convince his or her boss to sign the check that adds your work to their budget. It makes it easier for them to convince the marketing people, and for the marketing people to convince brick-and-mortar buyers to stock your book or give it floor space. Which makes it easier for people to see your book and decide to pick it up, and give it a chance.

At every step of the process, you are asking people to trust you. They'll find it easier if you've done the kind of hard work that means they *can* trust you. Much, much easier.

Not guaranteed, mind you. If there was a guaranteed magic wand to wave, I would be busy waving it instead of working my buns off and handing out advice. (Hey, I've got kids to feed.) Nothing is ever *guaranteed*. But you can up your chances, and it's foolish not to do so if you really, truly want to get published/an agent.

And that's pretty much all I can tell you.

The Myth of the Destructive Artist

October 24, 2008

Just a short writing post today, since I'm busier than a one-legged urban fantasy heroine in a leather-clad ass-kicking contest. (There are pumpkins to buy, after all.)

There's a new biography of Rimbaud out, which kind of got me thinking about what Julia Cameron calls (it may not be exact, but it's as I recall) the myth of the destructive artist. This is the cultural narrative that says artists are self-destructive, alcoholic, drug-addicted, or otherwise emotionally toxic.

This narrative shows up in the way we talk about creativity, biographies of creative people, and in the destruction some creatives seem to helplessly play out despite themselves. It seems against some sort of law to be a happy, healthy, reasonably well-adjusted creative.

I think a lot of this stems from the idea that creativity or making a living at creative pursuits somehow a violation of the Protestant work ethic. The creative life supplies "luxuries", this way of thinking goes, so it is evil and sinful and if you engage in it, you are evil and sinful too. The tension of this unconscious assumption is large enough to indeed drive you to drink.

The flip side to this is the idea that since you're already damned as an artist, you might as well go whole hog. A lot of artists/creatives do. There is also the implicit assumption of "all artists are like that", which excuses a lot of unhealthy interpersonal behavior—malignant narcissism, manipulation, double-dealing—all helped along by the idea that there are finite resources out there and artists have to fight tooth and nail for the lion's share of them, because otherwise they'll "lose".

If you want to be a productive creative over a long period of time—which is, to me, the point—I think you should take a look at this unspoken assumption and a very hard look at how it affects your own assumptions about the creative life.

Creativity is not a "luxury". It is a human birthright and a human need. You have a right to be creative, and you have a right to be a healthy, happy creative.

You also have a *responsibility* to take care of yourself so you can be one. Being a creative doesn't give you a "pass" when it comes to being a decent person. It's hard to let go of the myth of the automatically self-destructive artist, and equally hard to let go of the "oh poor me, I'm an *artist* so I can be an asshole to people." Both are stumbling-blocks that get in the way of doing your (perhaps self-chosen, but no less valid) job, which is producing art.

Being self-destructive doesn't make you an artist or a genius. It just makes you self-destructive, and lowers your chances of a long productive creative life.

There are valid reasons why people are self-destructive—abuse, trauma, social pressure, you name it. Therapy might be a good answer for that, and I'm not a licensed therapist. Art can even help you work through some of those issues, and it's a time-honored way to do so.

Blindly following the myth of the self-destructive artist not only cuts your chances of being a productive creative, it also cuts your chances of being a reasonably decent human being.

It's not that I think artists are under a higher constraint of decency[21] than everyone else—it's just that, with the massive power art has to affect the world, its purveyors are necessarily concerned with doing it the best they can. The myth of the self-destructive artist gets in the way.

---

[21] And please note that I am not using the word "decent" in the way prudes do, to beat free expression over the head. I am using it in the sense of: reasonably ethical, reasonably well-adjusted, reasonably reasonable—you get the idea.

On Truth, Close to the Bone

October 31, 2008

*I*never truckled; I never took off the hat to Fashion and held it
out for pennies. By God, I told them the truth."
                              Frank Norris, author of *McTeague*

Synchronicity gave me my Friday post this week. I
read the above quote in a book of Stephen King's essays
on writing, and thought *huh, I agree with that*. Then,
yesterday morning, my sister called. In the course of an
hour-long chat she asked if I ever felt like I was, well,
exposing myself too much in my books. If I ever felt scared
that I was showing too much and that people would know
me too well in them. Last night after tacos were eaten and
the kitchen (mostly) cleaned, my friend TrashGlam[22] and I
got on the subject of JT Leroy and the *Love and Consequences*
hoax. During the consumption of a bottle of very good red,
we moved on to the importance of Truth in fiction, what
constituted Truth, what did not, and various other things.

The job of any writer is to be as true as possible. A
memoir writer needs to stick closely to the Truth as we
think of it in our daily lives—the seasoning of personal
myth or personal perception of events should not be larger

---

[22] Yes, this is a pseudonym, in keeping with my commitment to
privacy.

than the serving of actual events that could theoretically be verified.

This sneaks up on a tricky question of human memory and personal mythologizing, which is not the point of this post. For the purposes of this essay, I am going to be using the word "truth" in several ways, and I'm going to be talking about the writing of fiction, not memoirs.

Okay, disclaimers done.

In *V for Vendetta*, Evie says "Artists use lies to tell the truth; politicians use lies to cover truth up." I agree with this wholeheartedly. The appeal of a novel or a character is largely how far the author permits herself[23] to tell the truth.

Of course I do not believe I am Dante Valentine, or Jill Kismet, or any other character of mine. On that path lies madness. But Dante, Jill, Japh, Perry, Kaia, Darik, and all the rest are true people to me. They are characters with flaws and strong points, and the things that happen to them are "real" and "true" insofar as I thought seriously about the world I had created, the consequences of such a world, and the consequences of their actions and personalities inside that world. These people are as real as I can make them, and they get hurt.

They are also, in some ways, aspects of questions and issues that concern me very much. Dante Valentine is on some level about my fear of abandonment and my issues with childhood abuse, not to mention religion, minorities, "chosen" family, and a host of other things. The Watchers and the Society series are me thinking about the problems of love, power, protection, drug addiction, and the justification (if any) of violence. Jill Kismet is about vigilantism, childhood abuse, prostitution, justification of violence—you get the idea. And all my stories hinge somehow on *redemption*. Even when I am writing to spec, writing with specific guidelines or salability in mind, *I* am

---

[23] Himself, herself, whatever.

writing about these issues and themes because they concern me as a human being.

Much of writing is, for me, a way to think about these issues, to hold a conversation with myself. But there is a deeper truth in here. The ending of *Working for the Devil* was so hard to write. I knew what the ending had to be, of course—I was pretty sure I was working on a series and had the framework in my head. The only way the framework would hold up is if a Certain Character died. I did not want that Certain Character to die. My editor did not want that Certain Character to die. My agent, my readers, nobody wanted that Certain Character to kick the bucket.

But he had to. Because it was the essential truth of the story, and I had made a bargain with the Muse and the story.

The bargain was I would not truckle. The bargain was I would tell the truth as best as I knew how, and the truth was that character had to die. There was no way around it. That was the way the story went.

I firmly believe writing is an act of faith, of magic, and of submission. The faith is that this thing, the work, is going to catch you when you fling yourself out into space. Committing wholeheartedly brings out a similar commitment from the work itself.

It is an act of magic because every act of creation is an act of magic, with all the power and mystery and danger that holds. It is an act of submission because you have to trust the work to know what it wants to be, and you cannot force what you think will sell better onto it. Forcing, let's say, a happy ending onto a story that doesn't have one is the height of bullshit, and readers will NOT stand for bullshit.

There is an implicit compact between me and the Reader when I set out. I commit to telling the story the best way I know how, and telling it truly. The Reader commits to suspending disbelief for a little while in order to be entertained, in order to enter my imagination and see this new world.

But there are dangers here. It is no less dangerous than the real world, "fiction" notwithstanding. People get hurt. There are monsters under the bed. To write a story is to call into service all the wonder and danger a human being is capable of, and Truth is not only the shield that protects but the blade that cuts.

This is entirely separate from the question of whether or not a Reader will like your book/story/whatever. We're not talking about personal tastes here. You can tell the story well and truly and there will still be people who don't like it. That's normal and natural. **But the chances of you reaching Readers who will like it goes up exponentially when you tell the truth. For the one thing Readers hate is to be bullshitted. To be lied to.**

BSing your Readers insults their intelligence, and when you've asked them to shell out hard-earned cash for your work and given them a handful of bullshit, do you wonder at their fury? If you tell the truth as best as you know how—staying true to the characters and the story— you will find your readers. A story with a ring of truth will find champions in the unlikeliest places. Your agent and editor will trust you and your story; their passion will get other people excited, and that's just for starters.

But it is so easy to lie. Why? Because, as I told my sister, *any* artistic creation is like stripping yourself naked and going out onto a busy street, screaming *Look at me! Look at me!* I am not saying it is exhibitionist. I am saying it is an act of marvelous emotional nakedness and vulnerability.

I'm sure there are people who think they know me because of the subject matter of my books. I'm sure there are people who feel a shock of kinship with something I've described, because they've been there and they know what it feels like. This is what I mean when I say "tell the truth." We are pressured to minimize or lie about several things in order to get along socially. In abusive families or relationships, we are outright forced to. *It's not that bad. It was your fault anyway. Quit crying. He doesn't drink that much. She didn't mean to break your arm.*

We are even shamed into feeling like we deserved it somehow, or like we will be ostracized if we dare to tell the things that happened to us. Every human being is fundamentally alone, and I think this is a huge impetus for art. Art is communication to bridge the gap between our fleshly selves. It is the congress of souls; it is the singing of one consciousness to another and the act of listening all in one.

This is what gives art its tremendous transgressive power. This is why making art is so emotionally fraught. We always think we are the only ones who have suffered this, or that (here's the big thing) *people will laugh.* I used to feel self-conscious in ballet class until I realized everyone else was equally self-conscious, and worrying about their own barre work to boot. Nobody would have time to worry about my jiggles or mistakes except the teacher, and it was the teacher's job to worry about those so s/he could tell me how to get better.[24] Everyone was too busy doing their own thing to care about mine. I was worrying over something that was almost nothing.

Still, the feeling one is going to be laughed at is a powerful deterrent to lowering our guard and getting emotionally naked on the page. To being vulnerable.

Make no mistake, there is vulnerability in art. I don't worry that people will "know" me anymore. I'm a complex person, and a simple one at the same time. I am a mystery wrapped in several riddles and even more engimas—just

---

[24] The feeling got better, but it has never entirely gone away. I do not think it ever will.

like everyone else. Any ammunition someone is going to find in my books is a risk I'm willing to take, and one I'm not overly concerned about.[25]

However. The Kismet books tear me up inside. Each one is a trip into a heart of darkness, and they require a lot of effort and work. I have to pay attention to them and really think about how to deal with this character and her world, how to tell her story honestly with no truckling...and when she is hit or hurt, I feel it. It exhausts me each time, and each time there comes a point in the story when I have to just let go and trust that the work is going to carry itself, that the book is going to finish itself, that all this will be worthwhile and not just wasted time and effort. That I haven't just been running around in circles barking at my own tail, so to speak.

It is very hard to trust. Especially in the face of vulnerability, the idea that people will laugh at you, or the naysaying voices in your head that ask you who the hell you think you are anyway, this isn't very good, it's stupid and—again—everyone is going to laugh at you.

Getting technically better—getting your grammar down, dealing with copyedits and revisions, etc.—is the easy part. Learning to take off your clothes every time and run down the street screaming is the not-so-easy part. Learning to take the risk of people pointing and laughing, learning to fling yourself out into space and hope like hell the story catches you... It's no wonder we're afraid.

But the feeling of having gotten to the end of the book, having done it honestly with no truckling, of having flung yourself out into space and had the strong and gentle hands of the divine work catch you and bring you safely to a landing on the other side...

---

[25] For a variety of reasons, not the least of which is the fact I'm writing **fiction**. Heh.

...that, my friends, is the purest magic. It requires much, but it gives so much more in return. And each time we stand on the other side of the work, breathing heavily and knowing we have finished, the glory of it is so big that we look back and think *well, that wasn't so bad, I worried for nothing.* Then we forget until next time.

Throwing yourself out there never gets any easier, but the joy of being caught never gets any less either. I guess there's a metaphor for life in there, but I'll be damned if I'm going to sit around wondering about it. Not when there's work to be done. *grin*

So, dear Reader and dearest fellow writers, here comes the most important part of this long rambling post. It's summed up in four little words. What do *you* think?

Suckage, Zero Draft, and Bicycles

November 7, 2008

First drafts—what I call a zero draft, because to me a first draft is one you can let someone else see—suck.

This is a law of writing.

I feel confident in asserting **there has never been a first draft that has not sucked**. Hemingway and Kerouac rewrote. So did Trollope, Dickens, Salinger, Wolfe, Eliot, and anyone else you care to name. Zero drafts suck, world without end, amen.

Why keep going? Why keep plowing through this thing if it ends up being a messy, untidy, nasty little pile of adverbs and passive voice? (There. I wrote *passive voice* instead of *passive verbs*. Proud of me yet? It was a struggle, I tell you.) Because you have to go through the suckage to get to the good part.

Zero drafts are where you're so excited by what you're doing that you're gabbling, your hands are moving around a lot, you're so jazzed you're actually spitting while you speak. It takes a while to get everything you're excited about OUT, so you can start the process of trimming and shaping. I suspect this happens in movies too. I've seen enough "Director's Cuts" to think the editing room, just like the revision process, is a boon.

They are different parts of the creative process—sketching and practicing before you paint. Doing daily ballet class and choreography runs over and over again before the dress rehearsal, before you get onstage. Practicing a speech in the mirror before you give it.

I don't know why writers think the book has to be perfect the instant it falls out of your head. Mostly, I suspect, because we only see the finished book on the shelves and publishing holds onto that air of mystique with claws and toenails. The mystique serves a number of purposes—but that's (say it with me) another blog post.

There is the biggest hurdle, the one I want to talk to you about. It's the Inner Censor, telling you to *quit this writing thing, you suck, nothing will ever get better and you'll never finish and oh, by the way, you're ugly too and nobody loves you.*

I have three little words for that. I can't say it any more simply than this: **FUCK THAT NOISE.**

The Censor's job is not to make your writing better. The Censor's job is to make you feel bad. Sometimes the Censor has something valuable to say— once in a blue moon, when the planets align and the right virgin sacrifices have been made and the armies have massed to conquer. (In other words, almost never.)

The Censor is not your Editor or your Conscience. It is the voice of everyone who ever told you that you were Not Good Enough, and as such it does not deserve to see the Zero Draft before everyone else does. Send Sven and Oleg after the Censor. I promise thee it shall do thee no harm, dearest fellow Writer.

Let me tell you a little story. When I was learning to ride a bicycle, they tried to tell me to pedal backward to stop. (It was one of those Huffy Pink Princesses with the chain-brake, not a hand-brake.) It didn't make any sense to me, so to stop, I would just pick something and run into it. Much injury (that I am now old enough to regard as hilarity) ensued. They would keep telling me to pedal backward, but it just didn't connect inside my head.

191

For those of you just joining us: Yes, I have always been this goddamn stubborn. I don't think it will change at this late date.

One day, something happened. It was like something lit up in another corner of my brain. I snapped the pedals back and stood on them, and produced a long, admirable skid mark. As if I'd been practicing braking all this time. It *suddenly* made sense to me.

Hang with me here. I find a lot of motivation in stubbornly telling my Inner Censor I'm going to do it DESPITE. Or just to spite, whichever. (Hey, you take it where you find it.)

Writing a zero draft is like being on that bicycle and having to run into things to stop. Getting tipped off and skinning various body parts. Being so excited by the sound of wind in your ears and the motion that you're not very good at first. But one day, the goddamn thing is finished. You snap the brakes back, produce a skid, and stand there for a second, smelling the good smell of outside on a sunny day and breathing deep, your whole body tingling. That's when you start riding the bicycle for revisions.

The finished book is when you're in the effing Tour de France. Only you're not riding to dope yourself up and beat out everyone. You're riding because of the wind in your ears and the feeling of the ribbon of the road unreeling under your tires.

The sucky thing is, each time you start a new project you have to learn how to hit the brakes all over again. It doesn't get much easier, but there is a certain amount of comfort in knowing the process. Knowing eventually that *click* in your head will happen.

Falling off the bike and running into things to stop sucks. It leaves bruises and it's hard. Zero drafts are messy and they suck. It leaves bruises too, and it's mega hard. But please don't stop. Learning to really ride that beast of a bicycle is worth it. The zero drafts suck, but it gets made up for later, I promise.

Now get out there and ride.

Don't Over-Chew That Steak, Sweetheart

November 14, 2008

I am now in that part of the novel—a quarter to a third through, basically—where I realize I have been wrong for twenty-odd thousand words and now I know the real way everything should go. This feeling is deep and panic-laden, and it is the bane of many a good writer.

The seduction, of course, is to go back over what you've written and rewrite it according to the New Shiny Idea. This is all very well, but it doesn't get one any further toward the finish line. My solution is to just start at that point, assume I can fix the front end of the book later, and write the rest of the story according to the New Shiny Idea. A zero draft does not have to be perfect, and **it's a lot easier to go back and tweak the initial 20K than it is to rewrite the first 20K five times and then get discouraged and toss the whole work, which usually ends up happening**.

Constantly reworking the front of your novel according to the New Shiny Idea is 98% of the time an avoidance tactic dressed up as something you could conceivably think is good writing habit. It *feels* like you're making progress, you end up writing 70-100K or so, but you do not have a finished work to show for it. You have an over-chewed piece of steak. It is a trick to keep you from finishing, because finishing is scary. Finishing is scary because it is only the first step in submitting, getting rejected or published, etc. It represents a whole new set of problems, chief among them is the ever-famous Internal Censor screaming *you finished this and it's still a piece of crap! Who told you that you could do this!*

I can't say it often enough. Do yourself a favor and get the whole corpse up on the table before you start operating on it, trimming and tweaking and making it pretty enough to bury. (Hey, all metaphors break down sooner or later. Sue me.)

Do not worry if you get a great idea of blinding flash of light a third or a quarter or half of the way there. Incorporate that idea *at* the point you get it, and keep forging ahead. Believe me, you will revise a finished work often enough to get sick of it, and enough times to fully meld that shiny idea seamlessly with the beginning.

Just don't obsessively rework the front end of the story. Of all the avoidance behaviors new (and even experienced) writers display, this is one of the worst and most seductive because it feels like you're doing actual work when you're really...not.

It's hard just to keep on keepin' on. Believe me. I am right now trying my damndest not to go back and fiddle with a few important things that ABSOLUTELY MUST go in the front of the story—but if they ABSOLUTELY MUST, I will catch them in revision. So will my beta, and my editor, and my agent. There will be no shortage of opportunities to shoehorn. Right now, though, my job is to get this whole thing out of my head and onto the page.

Time to get back to work

On The Self-Driven Writer

November 28, 2008

I hit 50K on my NaNoWriMo project last night—after the kitchen was cleaned up. (This is for book 2 of the *Strange Angels* series.) Just after that I finished reading Kage Baker's *The Graveyard Game*.

I went to bed feeling like a champion. It's a precious feeling. Often I feel like I'm just juggling fiery things; like it's all I can do to grab the next chainsaw as it starts to come down and send it back up. Part of this dynamic is simple— it's how I like it, when I'm running near full capacity I don't feel lazy.

Part of the dynamic is complex—a stew of work ethic plus fierce perfectionism and the thought that maybe if I work hard and fast and good enough "they" will love me. That component is a pure search for the approval I never had as a child, and it's so useful I have kept it even though it drives me crazy.[26] I don't know what I would be without driving myself so hard. I get a funny squirrelly feeling when I think of maybe not demanding as much from myself.

The dark side of it is this feeling that *I could be doing better no matter how hard I work*, which can tip one into a cycle of self-destructive chewing at the leather straps of life.

---

[26] The conscious choice to keep a particular response is different from suffering that response unconsciously and allowing it to fuck up your life. At least, that's my story and I'm stickin' to it.

While I don't quite advocate this for other writers (Jesus, who in their right mind would, even if it works for me?) I still think it is crucial for a writer to have an internal drive.

I will even go so far as to say this drive has to be higher than average. Nobody is standing over you with a truncheon *making* you write. An editor will not be calling you every day to see if you've gotten your wordcount in. You're expected to produce and turn in a reasonably finished product, because it's what you're contracted for.

The daily slog of writing work requires you to be your own boss; if you expect to make a living from writing you have to have not only the drive to make your craft better and deal with rejection but the self-imposed will to work every damn day to get the job done without someone poking at you.

It's a lonely road. I've worked in offices and I've worked retail; I've even worked in manufacturing. In each instance I could cope with having micromanagers, but I worked much better when I was given an objective and then left alone to do it.

This translated out very well to writing, but it was more of a handicap while working, say, retail. It was a big problem in office work. I wanted to give my best—but unfortunately, the manager wanted to "control" or wanted their emotional needs filled in a way that didn't mesh with me producing my best. Often (not all the time, mind you, but often) people get into management because they're good bureaucratic sociopaths. But that's another blog post.

Writing for a living requires a completely different set of skills than office work. Working retail is good for gathering material—Christ, is it *ever*—but the skills you develop there don't serve you in very good stead when it's just you and the keyboard and the blood-tinted sweat prickling on your forehead.

This is why when I say "writer" I'm referring to someone who wants to make a living from this thing, or at least have a reasonable chance of consistently getting published.[27] A lot of hobbyists call themselves writers; that's not a bad thing. But I do think there's a dearth of professional advice. A lot of people engage in speshul snowflakery or just plain obfuscation over writing.

Don't get me wrong. There is a mystery at the heart of every creative endeavor. That's why it's Creation. It's one of the biggest mysteries known to us. But there's also a paradox—hard work and discipline prepare the ground for that mystery (the harder I work, the luckier I get syndrome) and prepare the ground for making a living from that mystery.

Sculpting and painting require a certain amount of technical proficiency (don't throw "modern" art at me here, please); I don't know why people like to think writing is any different. That technical proficiency goes hand in hand with hard work and discipline. Making a living from writing requires hard work, discipline, technical proficiency, and creativity. It's no wonder it feels like juggling fiery chainsaws.

This is why I think NaNo is good for a lot of writers or hobbyists who think they might want to become writers. The process of having this kind of goal—brute output— and a deadline does wonderful things for those people suited to it. It can also teach a professional writer a refinement or two on the nature of their own creative and self-imposed drive. The skills and drive to become a professional writer, to make a living at this jazz, are not some collection of arcana only shown to those with the Golden Handshake. Like any skills, they can be practiced, learned, fiddled with, and tweaked for a particular personality or set of circumstances.

---

[27] Do not moan at me about how I don't have a trademark on the word "writer". I offer this definition so you know what I'm talking about, in the interests of being as precise and clear as possible. 'Nuff said.

Thinking about how you're going to solve the problem of being self-driven, how you're going to arrange things to get yourself through fifty thousand words or so, is immensely valuable. Great ideas are good. Practiced craft and discipline to convey those ideas is better, and is totally learnable. Practiced discipline and self-drive to get those ideas out into the world, to deal with submissions guidelines and editors and deadlines and copyedits and all that Other Stuff is the best of all, because the work isn't just languishing in isolation. It is out there doing what it's meant to do.

Each step in the process has its own rewards and pitfalls. Part of the joy of being self-driven is accomplishing a particular goal, like NaNo, and looking back over the peaks and valleys—and knowing you walked every inch of that alone. Knowing you pitted yourself against obstacles and pitfalls, and you came out ahead. Knowing you *did it*, goddammit, and every inch of that victory you sweated for is your own, your very own, your precioussssssss.

It is a wonderful feeling. It should be. Because tomorrow I'm going to have to get up and do it all over again, and if I don't feel good about it why on earth will I do it? Take your victories where you find them.

I think I'm going to celebrate by taking a walk. Or going out for Thai and getting a mojito. Or maybe just by lying on the floor and feeling like I've climbed a mountain and ironed all the wrinkles out of my cerebellum at once. It's a small triumph, perhaps. But it's all mine, and I'll take it.

Tomorrow it's back to juggling chainsaws. Today, however, it's feeling good about the fiery machines I've juggled so far.

Division of Labor,
Or, the Muse At My BonBons

December 5, 2008

I often say the characters do all the heavy lifting and I'm just the scribe. This is true as far as it goes, and like all true statements it is more complex than it appears.

To put it simply, there is a division of labor in this storytelling gig. I do my work, and the characters take care of themselves.

I am responsible for showing up at the keyboard every damn day. I am responsible for shutting out distractions and making writing a priority. I am also responsible for filling my creative "well" with images and Stuff. I am responsible for knowing the technical stuff—grammar and structure, etc.

The Muse is responsible for ideas, for characters, for the telling detail, and for vomiting up raw material for me to shape. (Pardon me a moment, I just had the image of a bulimic Muse and about laughed myself into a heart attack. Nobody else knows what's so funny. Story of my life.)

I do not ever worry about running out of ideas or characters or stories. That is not my job. They are lined up around the block and it's physically impossible for me to get to them all before I die, even if I write 24/7. Which I can't do because, you know, I have a *life*. At least, I have kids. Close enough.

I'm responsible for my end, and the Muse never falls through on hers. I firmly believe if you make writing a priority, if you make the time to sit consistently at the keyboard and keep your grammar and your metaphysical pencil sharpened, you will never have to worry about the Muse's end of the deal.

Yes, she is fickle—but like all good nymphs she is amazingly faithful in her fickleness. The stories will come. You can't stop them. They will inundate like the sea trying to gulp down Venice or Holland.

Your job is to build the dikes and keep them maintained so you can keep the canals at a reasonable level. (Yeah, I know this analogy breaks down. You still get the picture, good enough.) Those dikes are consistent hard work and keeping your knowledge of craft constantly sharpened. You can reclaim acres and acres from the sea that way, in little chunks of work spread out over every day.

Do not wait for the Muse. She waits on you, not the other way around. Yeah, you can throw the bitch a bonbon every now and again to keep her happy. But the first step— of showing up consistently at the keyboard with your grammar clean and your head full of random stuff gleaned from life—is all yours. She will show up when you do.

The more you show up, the more she learns to trust you. This trust is fragile; you can break it by choosing not to be consistent. Then, like any jilted Havisham, she will immure herself in a house you can't get into. And that sucks like a big sucking thing. But you can always tempt her out by showing up at the keyboard again. Consistently.

My Muse is a bitch. She really is. She's fickle, unendurable, demanding, flighty, and constantly throwing cute little shinies across my path to distract me. She's also a right dominatrix when a book really takes hold and all my spare RAM is taken up with *keeping up with her.*

But she always shows up. Every time I sit down and do my part of the job, she steps up. 100% of the time, she gives her all. Since she does...well, I'm not going to do any less.

Don't worry about losing ideas or running out of ideas. That's not your job. Your job is simple: show up consistently with your grammar and put your hands on the keyboard.

That's it. No golden handshake or soopah-sekrit magic wand. You do your job, and the Muse will slather you with enough magic for twelve. She'll spread it around like coconut oil on a roasting bodybuilder. She'll cake it like Baby Jane's aging face; she'll spread it around like bribes in corrupt oligarchy. She'll throw so much magic at you you'll have trouble keeping up. She is very good at her job. You only have to be *consistent* at yours.

And all that wonder is yours for the taking.

On Groups, Workshops, and Agendas

December 12, 2008

Let me begin by saying I know writer's groups, critique groups, and workshops do work for some people.

I know a few (far too few, IMHO, but that's beside the point) people have been helped by them. I don't dispute that under the proper conditions and with the proper safeguards, they can be safe and fun. So can cars, stand-up comedy, juggling, and sex.

But I don't attend workshops and I don't have a group. I very rarely (like once a year at OryCon) partake in a critique group. I am very wary of workshops and groups in general, just like I'm wary of writing "classes".

It's all because of ersatz jolts and agendas.

Writing is hard, and support and community are good. I don't dispute that. I do have what I consider a community, and a good beta reader. I find both invaluable—but it took me a long time to find either. I had to find people whose agendas matched mine. My agenda is to make rent as a professional writer, and to have as little bullshit as possible going on around my work. This means I have no time or patience for the usual "critique" group or workshop.

This is not the fault of the really earnest and dedicated people who organize or attend. It's the fault of the Speshul Snowflakes and predators, conscious or unconscious. It's also the fault of the "self-help" component of lots of classes, workshops, and groups.

Let's talk about that component first. I don't like self-help books for the same reason I don't like writing books, or the diet industry. If there was a magic bullet that let you do all these things without hard work, the billion-dollar industries would tank overnight.

While there might be one or two things of value in these books, people end up mistaking the effort of reading them for effort toward changing whatever it is they're unhappy about. It's an ersatz jolt people mistake for real work.

After a while it wears off, and you run to the bookstore, begging another self-help book to take your money and give you that jolt again. This is the trap.

Notice I do not dispute there is *some* use to self-help, writing, or diet books. But to my mind, that use is far outweighed by the risk of **mistaking the passive effort of reading for the active effort of doing the damn work**.

I fully admit to falling into this trap over and over again until I realized nothing was changing and got disgusted with the whole thing. Even now I feel the siren song of self-help or diet books. It's hard to resist that prettily-packaged temptation. I see a lot of talented and otherwise self-directed new/young writers getting caught in the trap of mistaking the emotional jolt of workshops or crit groups as a valid replacement for the thankless slog of writing every day, submitting and getting rejected, and just generally working your ass off for very little pay. Which, to be honest, is what writing is.

I view workshops and crit groups as a nice occasional *condiment*, but in no way comparable to the main course. So to speak.

I realize I come to this as a working writer with kids to feed. Mine is not the only writing "agenda". There are hobbyists, people who don't want/need to make a living but do want to get published, and then there are the Speshul Snowflakes. **Any time you have a group setting, you have people with different agendas.**

Not long ago I attended a writer meeting, and there I met the Beethoven Blonde. This was a woman who talked and laughed loudest when it came to the social part of the gathering, literally grandstanding and steamrolling over everyone else in the room. When it came time to read some pages, though, she had a ready excuse, flipping her long blonde hair back over her shoulder with an affected laugh.

"Well, I suppose I'm still *developing*. It just takes so much *time*, you know. I have to go *upstairs* to my room, where I can have absolute *quiet*, and then I turn on Beethoven and I *struggle* to *create*."

No shit. It's this kind of "writer" who gives the hardworking midlister—and creatives everywhere—a bad image.

And there are those people whose agendas are not about writing, per se. These are the people with emotional agendas who hijack groups and workshops. Suddenly the group/workshop is not about writing, it's about Them And Their Drama. They can get Passive-Aggressive, Abusive, Loud, or just plain Backstabbing And Horrid.

This is the largest reason why I don't do groups and workshops. I have seen too many of them get hijacked by a Speshul Effing Snowflake like the Beethoven Blonde. Or by the person who can't take honest crit because YOU DON'T UNDERSTAND THEIR GEEEEENIUS; the person who doesn't need an editor because editors only cramp their *style*, dontcha know; the person who is so avant-garde and groundbreaking that The Business Won't Understand Them—do I have to go on?

If you've attended a group or a workshop, I will bet you money you've encountered one of these, or one of the many others I could list.

These people waste a lot of time. In a group, they can be toxic because sharing one's writing is an emotionally vulnerable exercise. There are people who are writing and crit-group predators. (Any source of vulnerability/prey will draw them. This is just a fact of life.) If the group dynamics don't exclude them and exclude them HARD, they will destroy your group, do their best to destroy your peace of mind, and move on to the next feeding-ground. Many writers' groups have no boundaries when it comes to interpersonal behavior. Let's face it: critique can get *very* personal with *very* little provocation. It's a recipe for disaster.

With workshops, you get a slightly different class of predator—the predators who paid to be there just like the folks who honestly want to get writing practice/advice instead of drama out of the workshop. Forking over the cash does give them some rights, but not the right to completely hijack the workshop and behave inappropriately. If the people running the workshop don't watch and set boundaries (and refuse to take any shit), the situation quickly becomes unbearably toxic, and a complete and total waste of money and time for the people who really needed to get something other than drama out of it.

Because of the emotional component of writing, and because of the way we treat creativity and artists in our society, groups and workshops are playgrounds for predators, from the sad and pathetic passive-aggressive to the finely-tuned killing machine.

Writing groups implode regularly from this type of stress; so do crit groups. Perennial workshop attendees can be predators, deadweight, or people mistaking the drama and ersatz jolt of a workshop for real work. The chance of drawing a decent writing group or attending a workshop that won't get hijacked is, to my mind, analogous to the chance of winning the lotto or having an airplane part fall out of the sky onto your head. It CAN happen, sure. But my money is on writing every day and getting to the point where you can spot the people with Emotional Agendas, not writing agendas—and AVOID THEM LIKE THE FRICKIN' PLAGUE. Then you're ready to sift through your community, online or not, and find a good beta reader or a nicely-balanced group, if you really think you need one.

Community is a wonderful thing. I have a great one, and I have a beta reader who is worth her weight in gold. Literally. (Yes, Selkie, I'm talking about you.) It took me over a decade to find my beta, and I had to function as a professional, largely on my own and without a community, for a long time before I did.

If you need a group, if you really think you need workshops, fine. If that works for you, go for it. Just be careful and watch out. It's a dangerous jungle out there.

Good luck.

On Depth and Reviews

Yesterday I asked for ideas for this Friday post, and you responded in droves. Two questions kind of stood out—one about depth, and the other about reviews.

Reader (and fellow writer) Jessica Corra sent me this question: *I'd be interested on your take on making a story deeper. I've finally wrangled the craft beast to the point I am finishing novels (two in 2008, as soon as I write that blasted climax... *wink*) consistently, and the first one I subbed got positive feedback. But while I have now shown myself I can write an entertaining and coherent book, I am of course not satisfied. If I'm going to play the publishing game, I want to take it to the next level. I want depth, breadth, meaning. Got anything for me?*

Short answer: One is never finished with this question.

Long answer: Depth, breadth, and meaning are largely subjective.

That being said, there are a couple ways to get what I think you're after. First, you've finished novels. CONGRATULATIONS. This is a huge milestone. Do not underestimate how huge a thing this is.

Now for the bad news. It is now the real work begins. The first thing I do when I finish a book or a piece is **close it and walk away**. Celebrate a little. For short stories I can take a day or so off, novels get a week to three weeks (generally) of just sitting while I work on something else, drool into the carpet, catch up on reading—anything to calm down the creative engine and let the piece "cool off".

Finishing a novel feels to me very much like there is a huge flywheel inside my head that has now come unmoored and is spinning wildly, attached to nothing. It has to slow down and stop making that ratcheting sound before I can relax. By that point I'm sick of the piece, whatever it is. It has to go away for a while.

The hard part begins when you go back and start exercising the critical-reading muscles instead of the just-plain-vomit-it-out muscles. It requires a different sort of discipline. I usually go over every piece at least twice before the beta reader sees it, and it gets a thorough pick from the beta before it goes to an editor.

This takes time and hard work. For one thing, it's ridiculously hard to view your own words with the necessary distance. (Part of the cooling-off period is to hopefully get some of that distance.) For another, you can sometimes see the events so clearly in your head, you don't get critical bits of it on paper—you may need another set of eyes for that. (This is why I feel my beta is INVALUABLE.)

It may not seem like I'm answering your question, but I am. Just in a roundabout way, leading up to this: if you build it, Grasshopper, the themes will come.

Most of the time I am oblivious to any Deep Themes in my own stuff. It takes the beta or the editor saying, "Huh, I see you're really thinking about _____." And I say, "Yeah, I was, but I didn't think it bled into the book!" Then they laugh at my bafflement.

Any piece of work where you're being honest will have its own depth. Finding the way to bring that out is tricky. You can fall in love with your own soapbox, or let it get in the way of tellin' a whoppin' good story. It's a variant of bullshitting, and it's a kiss of death.

There are things that can help you, though. One of them is being mean to your characters. Do not shy away from their pain, from hurting them. If there is no risk, there is no reward for them OR for the Reader. Good stories are risky—like Samwise says in *The Two Towers* movie. Being too afraid to put your characters through the wringer, to risk them and yourself and your Reader...well, this line of work ain't for the fainthearted.

Another thing that can help you is reading. I am always amazed at "writers" who claim not to read. I agree with Stephen King (his *On Writing* is one of the two writing books I will ever recommend, period) that reading a lot is how you get taught subtle and numerous things about voice, pacing, why a book works, etc.

A funny thing happens when you read a lot as a writer. You start looking "under the hood", as the Selkie says, to see what makes a story go. You start noticing things— thinking *I would've solved that problem differently* or *O I SEE WHAT U DID THAR*! This whole dynamic has made me a much pickier reader, and I kind of miss that uncritical period where I swallowed books whole, bad good or indifferent. The glut started to teach me a *lot* about writing, and my beta and editors commented that my work got better. Deeper. Because I had a wider grasp of the mechanics and was no longer wrestling with the clutch and the brake; I was starting to focus on other parts of driving.

Another thing wide reading will do is teach you What You Like. Take a look at books you do like, books you don't feel the need to look under the hood of while you're reading. See if you can look at them like an editor would. Chances are you'll find Themes, and chances are those Themes are things you resonate with. Those Themes will start popping up more and more in your own work. The depth will happen.

What I hear from your question is you're in one of those uncomfortable periods (a plateau, as it were) right before your writing takes a big leap forward. This is part of the creative process, and one of the most frustrating parts.

The leap will happen if you keep working. Trust in that.

On the other hand, after the leap is another plateau...and another leap...and another—you get the idea. This sort of cycle never ends.

That's probably not the most useful answer in the world, but it's all I can give. For now.

The second question is about "voice" in reviews, and comes from a fellow LJer and writer, who has requested to remain anonymous. Parts of the in-depth question below are redacted, for obvious reasons.

We were talking about something else, and "voice" in reviews came up. The short answer I gave to this person's question ran thus: *Voice is crucial in any form of writing, I can't see why reviews would be any different.* No review is completely objective, of course; but that elusive quality of voice comes when a writer is being honest (a phrase that means several different things to me, many of which are applicable here). It damn near shines through, and often people will pick the less-bullshit, more-honest voice even if it doesn't agree with them—in fiction and in reviews.

The important codicil to this is that people tend to pick reviewers who either agree with them or who have tastes similar to theirs, like friends. A reviewer's stock may fall with even the readers who have a lot invested in them because of the similarity of taste and outlook, if the reviewer starts betraying the implicit covenant between reviewer and reader—or even fiction writer and reader.

That covenant is to tell the truth. (There's that phrase again.) It's not just you. The first reviewer's tastes may have changed, yours might have, they might have started bullshitting, or you guys may just disagree. Or you may have found a voice you like better. It's not just you, but there are many reasons why you might be going to a new place.

In reply I got this deeper, more precise explanation[28]: *"To expand on my question regarding voice in a review, I used to read **Famous Review Blog** religiously. While their reviews didn't really sway me one way or the other regarding my book buying habits, I did enjoy reading their reviews. They were analytical and thought-provoking, and provided a nice critical analysis of the book. Not nearly as entertaining as the **other Famous Review Blog**, but expansive and interesting.*

"It's probably just me, but over the past couple of months, I felt the voice of the reviews, especially by *_____* and *_____*, devolved. They seemed less of a review and more of an exercise in proving how sophisticated and highly educated they are. Honestly, the reviews became dull and tiresome because of it.

"Thing is, I knew these women were smart, educated and could provide great insight not only into individual books but into the publishing industry from the reader's perspective. I was there to read interesting, well thought out reviews, not be bludgeoned with some kind of weird one-upmanship regarding IQ scores thinly veiled by a book review. The voice changed—at least for me.

"I'd never mention this in a public post as **Famous Review Blog** is well-known and well-liked and has a rabid fan base that sometimes works with the pack mentality when defending their favorite review site from those they perceive as even the mildest threat or detractor. I don't want the hassle or the enemies and actually hope to use **Famous Review Blog**'s reviews some day for the exposure.

"Anywho, the above is the thought process that motivated my question. I'd be VERY interested in your take on the power of "voice" in a review."

Hmmm. That's a pickle. To get a little bit more specific...it must be some kind of internet law that any collaborative site, once it passes a certain critical threshold

---

[28] Which I was given permission to post, redacted to protect identities etc. Just so that's clear.

of popularity, will become (to varying degrees) the home of that sort of rabid us-against-them fanbase.

Review sites...well, reviews are opinions, and one must already believe one's opinions are worthwhile in order to go to the trouble of spending the time and care needed to run a review site. That belief can become pathological. In any creative endeavor (and reviews, I think, definitely count) there is the danger of believing one's own publicity. That gets sticky.

It seems like this is less a question of voice and more a question of bullshit. The one-upmanship you've noticed isn't "voice". It's either covering up weird insecurity or it's just plain nastiness, and either is damaging to any case a reviewer's building.

Readers hate to be belittled, to have their intelligence insulted, or to be bullshitted. (Bullshat? What *is* the proper past tense of "to bullshit" in that sentence?) The aroma of BS will drive away Readers faster than anything else. And a review site with that sort of dynamic going on runs a very real risk of becoming simply a mutual congratulation society with some weird and unhealthy behaviors. Either said site will change, become less popular, or it will implode. Or it may get more popular than ever with people who think reviews are all about tearing people down and not about giving an honest opinion and sparking discussion.

This is a thorny question for me, for obvious reasons. I have for a long time pursued a policy of not responding to reviews, either positive or negative.[29]

The problem with responding runs thus: even if you only respond to the positive ones, that astronomically ups

---

[29] If I am ever tempted to respond, I have to take 24 hours and ask someone whose opinion I trust. Usually it only takes me about twenty minutes to discover no, I really don't want to respond. Thus I am saved the trouble.

the chance of you someday responding personally to a negative one. DANGER, WILL ROBINSON! Doing *that* is one of the surest, shortest ways to an internet pileup that might be fun to watch but is so, so not fun to be a part of. (Example: the Anne Rice kerfluffle on Amazon a while ago.) Who needs that? Just avoid the whole thing.

I do read reviews of my work, negative and positive. (I don't see how any writer can avoid doing that, and feedback is good.) I may even (shhh!) moan privately to my beta or my close trusted friend about one or two of the negative ones. But publicly responding, even to positive ones? Hell no. That's not my job and it will only create stomach trouble for me. *puts tongue in cheek*

When all is said and done, really, it's just the internet. Heh. This has spread to me not reading much in the way of reviews unless I really, really trust and enjoy the site. And truly my TBR pile is so huge and reviews will only tempt me to add to it. And I'll be crushed under a pile of books. While that may be one of my Top Ten Ways To Die, I can't afford to do it right now. I have deadlines. Ergo, I am perhaps not the best person to ask about reviews, really.

More Thoughts on Angry Chicks in Leather

December 27, 2008

The Angry Chicks In Leather post[30] got a few comments.

The anonymous/troll comments fell into two categories: one, that I was a Bad Feminist (in several senses at once, from "shrill harpy" to "traitor to femininity") and that smaller, more delicate women couldn't kick ass; and two, that authors like Charles de Lint and Emma Bull and Jim Butcher were *true* Urban Fantasy and the stuff I was talking about was just lowbrow schlock.

Thanks for making my point for me on both counts, trolls.

I actually consider Charles de Lint and Emma Bull magical realists, not urban fantasists. (And China Mieville I consider steampunk fantasy, but that's just me.) They also published a lot earlier than the current spike of titles I consider urban fantasy, and in any case I defined my terms pretty thoroughly—urban fantasy as the chicks-in-leather flood we're having right now. There are exceptions like Jim Butcher's Harry Dresden (which to me seems more

---

[30] http://fantasyhotlist.blogspot.ca/2008/12/ad-lib-column-lilith-saintcrow.html

straight fantasy than urban fantasy, cityscape notwithstanding, for a variety of reasons).

The borders between urban fantasy, steampunk fantasy, straight fantasy with urban elements, some brands of magical realism, and paranormal romance are FLUID. They are not SOLID. Genre is more an ad hoc designation by bookstores than anything else, because you have to be able to *find* a book to *sell* it to the person who *wants* it.

Genre is also something for fans to argue about, because let's face it, fandom isn't fun without feuds[31]. Genre is also a set of conventions that give a writer some shape to aim for, somewhere to aim the arrow.

What genre isn't is this: a straitjacket. Or a way to denigrate someone else's experience. I made it pretty clear I was talking about the current wave of books designated urban fantasy. I gave my definitions and some of the reasons why I think this type of book is so "hot" right now. I also passionately defended it, because I think this genre is important and I *do* think there's a lot of social conversation going on under the surface in these books— conversations about sex, violence, justice, gender, expectations, identity, a whole kit and caboodle of issues.

These issues are not the story. Part of telling a good story (to answer the concern trolls who bleated "what happened to just telling a good *stoooory?*") is telling a **relevant** story. These are issues we're thinking about now, as a society. Just like *Star Trek* and hard sci-fi took on issues relevant to their day (and hard sci-fi still does) and high fantasy took (and takes) on issues relevant to their day through the lens and filter of genre, so too does urban fantasy.

Only we're not supposed to analyze or talk about it, either because these are scary taboo subjects...or because

---

[31] If you can't tell that's tongue in cheek, this is the wrong blog for you.

we're getting Too Big For Our Britches, because we only write schlock, dontcha know.

Yeah. Sure.

A lot of commenters also scoffed, saying chicks kicking ass wasn't a recent invention in Litrachur. Sure, there have been strong female protagonists in fiction for a long time. But the scale of the examination of women, violence, and guilt (or lack of it) urban fantasy engages in is a new bag, I think, because the women aren't portrayed as Bad or as Guilt-Racked over using violence. These female protagonists who are using violence are also not getting what I call the Bad Girls In Movies treatment—this is the principle that any sexually active (or *perceived* to be sexually active) woman in the movies will either be killed, redeemed (translated: her sexuality co-opted) by the (male) hero, or horribly disfigured.

Strong female protagonists in fiction have overwhelmingly been seen through the lens of the male.[32] (I know I'm simplifying the problem here for the sake of argument. Bear with me—not least because litrachur has overwhelmingly been a male pursuit in Western history, mmmkay?)

Urban fantasy seems to be examining these questions of power, violence, sex, and gender *through the lens of the female*, or at the very least not penalizing the female protagonists for utilizing violence.

---

[32] Like I said yesterday, don't even fucking pull up the straw man about how I must "obviously" hate men. I LIKE men. I've dated quite a few, married one, gave birth to one, and am raising two. I like men a lot. That doesn't mean I can't analyze gender roles and pressures in my own goddamn culture. Any comment dragging up that straw man in whatever form will be nuked without warning. Nuff said.

This creates spaces of ambiguity, which is why I think so many urban fantasy novels feel "noir".[33] This is also why plenty of urban fantasy novels have **explanations of how** a female protag gets jacked-up/superhuman strength or speed, or how they're arranged with the protag out-thinking/outsmarting the bad guys. This is a problem every UF author with a female protag has wrestled with and solved with varying degrees of finesse and success.

It is the methods of wrestling and solving, I think, that make UF so cool. Those methods also show a lot about attitudes toward violence and justice, and allow the writer (consciously or unconsciously) to slip in a theme or two. This is no different than, say, Thackeray showing attitudes about social climbing or hypocrisy by picking the type of protagonist and structure that he did. Or Dickens showing attitudes toward poverty, criminality, and morality by picking the protagonists and plots that he did. Or Heinlein showing attitudes toward sexuality, intelligence, and social organization by—you get the idea. *All* writers do this with varying degrees of relevance and success.

Telling a good story doesn't mean your work has to be free of thought or themes. Themes will creep up and insert themselves in your work without you knowing. It's the nature of the beast. I'm excited about these themes being examined in these ways, and I think it's important.

Yes, there's drek in UF. There's also drek in Litrachur. Sturgeon's Law applies equally to both. But even pulp, schlock, and Bad Trashy Lowbrow stuff can tell us oodles about our social attitudes, what we consider important, and how those attitudes are shifting and changing over time. Genre fiction is valuable even if you and I disagree over it being lowbrow, and who the fuck cares if it's lowbrow

---

[33] My analysis of "noir" as characterized largely but not exclusively by moral and ethical ambiguity is known. In the interests of space conservation, I will pass over making that case in-depth.

anyway? *People* are reading it because it resonates with them, and the treatment of violence and gender expectations in UF is one of the big reasons why I think so MANY people are reading it now. It's "hot" right now for Reasons.

I've explained one of those reasons, to my way of thinking. The floor's open for you to explain yours. *grin*

About the Author

Lili lives in Vancouver, Washington, with two dogs, two guinea pigs, two cats, two children, and a metric ton of books holding her house together. However, referring to her as "Noah" will likely get you a lecture.

Also by Lilith Saintcrow